BUILDING A BETTER M

Building a Better Man presents a theory and science-based discussion of masculinity in modern America, but it also does much more than that—it interweaves a diverse group of compelling personal stories with an exploration of aggression and masculinity in the socialization of boys and men. Where other programs tend to subtly denigrate men as perpetrators and focus on stopping the problematic behavior, *Building a Better Man* tries to understand the external forces that impinge on the developmental experiences of boys/men and broadens the scope of inquiry into their behavior by reviewing a range of external societal forces that contribute to the problems. Clinicians and group leaders will find that the approach laid out in *Building a Better Man* leaves clients feeling understood more than judged, which provides a different motivation for change and can set treatment on an entirely different and infinitely more productive path.

William Seymour, PhD, is a licensed psychologist working at Children's Hospital of Wisconsin and an assistant clinical professor at the Medical College of Wisconsin.

Ramel Smith, PhD, is a licensed psychologist and president of BLAQUESMITH Psychological Consultative Services, LLC, in Milwaukee, Wisconsin.

Héctor Torres, PsyD, is a licensed clinical psychologist and an associate professor at the Chicago School of Professional Psychology.

BUILDING A BETTER MAN

**A BLUEPRINT
FOR DECREASING
VIOLENCE AND
INCREASING
PROSOCIAL
BEHAVIOR IN MEN**

William Seymour, Ramel Smith, and Héctor Torres

Routledge
Taylor & Francis Group

NEW YORK AND LONDON

First published 2014
by Routledge
711 Third Avenue, New York, NY 10017

and by Routledge
27 Church Road, Hove, East Sussex, BN3 2FA

Routledge is an imprint of the Taylor & Francis Group, an informa business

© 2014 William Seymour, Ramel Smith, and Héctor Torres

The right of William Seymour, Ramel Smith, and Héctor Torres to be identified as authors of this work has been asserted by them in accordance with sections 77 and 78 of the Copyright, Designs and Patents Act 1988.

Library of Congress Cataloging in Publication Data
Seymour, William, 1959–
    Building a better man : a blueprint for decreasing violence and increasing prosocial behavior in men / by William Seymour, Ramel Smith, and Héctor Torres.
       pages cm
     Includes bibliographical references and index.
    1. Men–Psychology. 2. Masculinity. 3. Violence in men. I. Smith, Ramel. II. Torres, Hector, 1975– III. Title.
    HQ1090.S46 2014
    155.3'32–dc23
                                     2013050293

ISBN: 978-0-415-70826-5 (hbk)
ISBN: 978-0-415-70827-2 (pbk)
ISBN: 978-1-315-88615-2 (ebk)

Typeset in Dutch823 BT
by Keystroke, Station Road, Codsall, Wolverhampton

CONTENTS

FOREWORD
Frederick Marx

Men are made, not born. We tend to think in this society when a male reaches 18 or 21, graduates high school or college, has that first drink or sexual experience, drives a car or joins the army, or, worse, robs or steals, rapes a woman or takes a daredevil risk, beats up a "sissy" or shoots someone, that he is now miraculously a man. These and related notions are some of the most pernicious yet commonplace in our society today. The repercussions of this ignorance could not be more far reaching. They are everywhere to behold. We live in an age where suspended adolescence seems to be the norm for all too many men, most notably among men in positions of power.

Indigenous cultures knew better. For them there was no such thing as adolescence. You were either a child or an adult. To mark that threshold, to perform and accomplish that transformation, was a function of the village itself. It was a cultural obligation. Biology alone would not do it. Village elders, both men and women, accepted the responsibility their ancestors entrusted them with. The African proverb summarizes this neatly: "If we do not initiate the young they will burn down the village to feel the heat."

But how can we even aspire to universal values of mature masculinity when we inhabit a world so varied by culture, race, class, religion, nationality, sexual preference, age, and more? I believe we can, as do Doctors Seymour, Smith, and Torres. The key of course is not to ignore difference or go around it, but to go *through* difference. Once we acknowledge and name our deep and significant differences, we can begin to open our hearts to what unites us as men, not in spite of but because of those differences, what makes it possible to proudly and without exaggeration recognize ourselves as brothers. "Brothers from another mother," as some put it. Or, as Asa Baber wrote:

> *Each man is my Father*
> *Each man is my Brother*
> *Each man is my Son*
> *Each man is my Leader*
> *Each man is my Teacher*
> *Each man is my Mirror*
> *I will always remember it*

I will always honor it
I will always accept it
My pledge is to men
To their safety and growth
My work is for men
And life is my goal

This is the invitation and promise that these three men hold open to us. The rawness and pain reflected in their own shared stories is the portal. They model for us the road men must walk. Into the grief, into the shadows, into the truth and acceptance. But the promise of living life happier, more fulfilled, more connected and at peace is what lies in wait if only men have the courage to accept.

It is one of the most significant invitations of our time. If you're a man reading these words, I trust you have already said yes. If you're a woman reading these words, I trust you'll take them to heart for the men in your life. Welcome.

Frederick Marx
Filmmaker/Writer **BOYS TO MEN?**,
JOURNEY FROM ZANSKAR, and **HOOP DREAMS**
RitesofPassageMovie.com

PREFACE

As part of our Building a Better Man workshops, we asked participants to reflect on issues of masculinity and violence and to share their advice in a letter to a young person about becoming a better man. These letters are so powerful and perceptive that we included one at the beginning and end of this preface.[1] They represent the emotional soul searching our participants go through during the intervention and are inspiring examples of how strength, courage, and wisdom have built better men.

Dear Little Man,

This is a letter from yourself, but now you are 35. Despite what you think, you are not a pro-football player or a lawyer. You never went to Notre Dame and played football. So you need to listen to what I am about to tell you.

Right now you are 35 years old, father of two children and an addict. Needless to say, you are not what you expected. You need to understand that it wasn't hard to get here, it probably was the easiest thing you have ever done. Addiction has led to many of your problems. You never finished school 'cause of drugs. You committed many burglary 'cause you were high. You are in and out of jail till you hurt someone, and then you are in prison. At that point, you take a lot out of life and do good for years. Somewhere you relax and next thing you know, you are selling drugs to support your habit, and next thing I am writing this letter.

You are a tough person, this I know. Everything I have said is the easy part. The difficult part is the part about the people around you. Your family that you are torn away from 'cause of your choices. You will find out your family life doesn't go how you think it will. It is hard to deal with the hurt you cause them and the missed holidays. You missed out on a lot of time with grandpa. Yes, he passes away before you are 32. Your brother loses a leg, and you don't find out for two years after it happens.

When you get older you make a promise to yourself that if you have children, that they won't grow up like you. Well, right now there are two beautiful kids at home asking when is daddy going to come home. Those children don't deserve that. Just like you didn't deserve what happened to you during your childhood. Dealing with that pain and the pain you have caused your family is the hardest thing you will deal with in life. Even at 35 you don't know how to deal with it. At times you feel like you are just going to lose it. It is so intense that you feel like you are going to tear apart in the chest from the hurt. I know in my heart it doesn't have to be this way. Your family is there for you. Don't be too proud and leave that "I can take care of it myself" attitude behind. They are not offering you charity. They are offering you love. It is hard to let go of that independent attitude but it is harder to deal with life without their support.

I hope you are able to understand the power of this letter because I am just starting to do so myself. There are people who love you out there and will be there for you. You don't have to turn to drugs, crime, or violence to live like a man. Let go of yourself and ask for help 'cause you will get it with no regrets or resentment toward you. Remember it is not a hand-out they are offering, it is a hand-up!! Fill your heart with love.

Yourself, 35 years

In 2007, we (Drs. Seymour, Smith, and Torres) met in a coffee shop to discuss a shared concern. The three of us had been working with young males and were perplexed by the overwhelming number of violent youth offenders referred to us who had been impacted by trauma and responded with "anger" and "aggression." This trend was not isolated to our caseloads but was occurring throughout the United States, as evidenced in the media's constant coverage of regrettable violent incidents.

As we continued to discuss our concerns, we navigated through intricate layers of influence that contributed to violence. We realized this issue was multifaceted and complex. We found ourselves in frequent disagreement about what measures would prevent and decrease violence among young males. Each of us brought a different viewpoint, which initially appeared to be in opposition to that of the others. This was not a surprise; as you read through our stories in Chapter 1, you will see that our lives had been extremely different prior to that conversation. Our diverse socioeconomic, racial, ethnic, sexual orientation, and academic backgrounds, not to mention our respective life experiences, had led each of us to think about the problem of violence from a markedly dissimilar perspective. However, it did not take long for us to see the common denominator in our arguments—masculinity hegemony. Though we each had a slightly varied definition of the concept, we were able to clearly identify masculinity socialization as the intersecting factor that connected us—males—to our relationship with anger, aggression, and violence.

As boys and young men, we were all brought up according to similar standards of masculinity. Although our backgrounds and environments were radically different, similar societal standards of what it means to be a man and how a man should behave were ingrained in us. The messages we received at home, at school, from community leaders, and in the media prescribed the way a man was expected to act.

In 2008, after months of meetings and conference calls, Building a Better Man was born. Since then, the main goal of our work has been to employ our narratives, generate dialogue, and implement eclectic interventions within a foundation of cognitive behavioral techniques. In our efforts to decrease violence among participants in our program, the key aspects of our mission became clear:

1. As a society we need to broaden and internalize a new definition of masculinity that incorporates alternate views of what it means to be a man.

2. Males need to advance from a place where they are unaware of their male privilege to a place where they take action based on their awareness of the issues related to that power and privilege.

3. Men need to address their intrapersonal deficits and understand the "*ene-me*" inside themselves that produces preventable violent acts and situations.

4. Males can greatly benefit from improving their interpersonal and coping skills.

5. It is important for men to engage in prosocial activities and contribute to their communities.

6. In addition to avoiding the use of violence, men must be accountable for their male privilege and seek justice in all interpersonal interactions.

7. A solution to the violence epidemic requires the participation of all involved, as the solution is systemic and ecological in nature.

Building a Better Man: A Blueprint for Decreasing Violence and Increasing Prosocial Behavior in Men provides the theoretical and empirical foundation of our intervention. It provides the tools and recommendations that educators, mental health and social service providers, and parents need to initiate a productive dialogue on the issue of masculinity and violence in different settings.

Part I of this book, "Laying the Groundwork," begins with our personal stories, which illustrate how our backgrounds influence who we are as men. We each describe our unique challenges growing up, the intersection of our identities, and the continual process of how we develop our sense of masculinity, even today. Our stories serve as a starting point for a dialogue on masculinity in modern America, and we believe they can also serve as tools to initiate discussions about topics such as race, ethnicity, sexual orientation, and privilege. Chapter 2 provides statistical, historical, and anecdotal evidence of how young males contribute to systematic violence and antisocial behavior. We emphasize the importance of evaluating the socialization of males with respect to violence in society and why it is critical for parents to raise boys with a healthy range of emotion. Chapter 3 presents our Masculinity Developmental Hierarchy model, which outlines the three stages males go through in their transition from a formative state, holding conventional notions of masculinity and endorsing a restrictive view of gender roles, to the acceptance and adoption of a broader, healthier view of masculinity.

Part II of the book, "Building from the Ground Up," teaches skills that the reader can take away and use in daily life, with an emphasis on the three I's: intrapersonal, interpersonal, and involvement. Chapter 4 provides an overview of the violence prevention literature, including strategies and practices that have proven to be effective in reducing violence, particularly those that have been effective among men and that address issues of diversity. Chapter 5 outlines our eight week intervention; progressing from guiding philosophy to sequential sessions that are practical, strength-based, action-oriented, and based on a cognitive-behavioral and positive masculinity approach to individual and group intervention in our three areas of focus (intrapersonal, interpersonal, and involvement in community). Chapter 6 describes a broader community application of the intervention, integrating multiple change agents and centers of social influence grounded in a preventative, ecological approach to generational violence. Finally, Chapter 7 provides ten recommendations for how individual men can address issues of masculinity and violence on their own. It also describes an approach for parents (both mothers and fathers) who are motivated to help their sons broaden their definition of masculinity and prevent/reduce antisocial or violent behavior.

We would like to acknowledge our families for their patience and support, not only with this project but for putting up with such imperfect men and having the patience to accompany us in our own journey to become "better men." A special acknowledgment goes to the boys, young men, and adults we have worked with who were brave enough to reveal what was behind their masks and show us who they really were—vulnerabilities and all. This is particularly true for the men in the Wisconsin correctional system who, despite their difficult situation, had the courage to engage in our workshops with open hearts. Their stories and lessons were moving and changed us. We hope our intervention served as their first step toward becoming better men.

Dear men,
What are you waiting for?
Now that you are aware that there is,
A dream for you to follow,
A goal for you to set,
A project for you to make,
An idea for you to act on,
A possibility for you to explore,
An opportunity for you to grab,
A place for you in your community,
A network of selected people that will support you,
A choice for you to make.
A responsibility to be a better man,
For your loved ones, your community, but most of all for you.

Alejandro, 16 years old

NOTE

1   The letters and identifying information have been slightly modified to protect the writers' identities.

PART I

LAYING THE GROUNDWORK

1

THREE MEN, THREE STORIES

A memory is what is left when something happens and does not completely unhappen.

Edward de Bono

HÉCTOR'S STORY

Mis Raices: My Roots

To state that I was born in San Juan, Puerto Rico, is not the beginning of my story. Before my arrival, my extended family had already endured a long history of hardship that included family deaths due to lack of resources and violent accidents, absence of family members due to participation in the military and wars, and extreme poverty, among other things. Living and surviving chronic hardship leaves deep scars that go beyond those who experience it, and are transmitted to subsequent generations.

When I think of adjectives to describe my family that may have resulted from coping with the past, I think of these: enthusiastic, emotional, strict, distressed, nervous, wounded, grateful, complaisant, apprehensive, resourceful, resilient, proud, caring, and loving. I am privileged that by the time I arrived in this world, the economic situation of my family was much better and I did not have to experience the extreme lack of economic resources that those before me faced. My challenges were of another nature.

My paternal and maternal grandparents lived in Ponce. The city of Ponce is located in the south of the island, approximately 75 miles from San Juan, Puerto Rico's capital. People from Ponce tend to be conservative, traditions are important, Catholicism is very prominent, and connections with others are greatly valued. Both sets of grandparents were from mixed races with humble backgrounds; they were working class, very ethical, and traditional individuals.

My family is an important part of my story, as Latino cultures tend to be family-centered. In the research literature, we tend to call that familismo.[1] In part, this means that collective needs are greater than those of a single individual in the family; that individuals' decisions have an impact on the whole family (and vice versa), and there is an expectation that family members will be close and rely on each other. Another implication is that everyone in the family has a role and responsibility, and there is an expectation to mutually respect each other's role in the family hierarchy. The man is the chief of the family, who provides and rules. The woman is responsible for the household, including children's discipline and the family's spiritual well-being. The children must respect, follow order, never interrupt, and learn from their parents so that they can replicate this system in their future families. My family did accordingly. My grandmothers took care of the family, my grandfathers were the breadwinners, the female children helped around the house, and the boys played sports, fixed things, did heavy lifting, and did other "manly" things, including learning how to be served and taken care of.

Each of my parents was the youngest among many children. They married and had their first two children, my siblings, in Ponce. At the time my mother was pregnant with her third child, me, my father was offered a job in San Juan. Although today there is a highway that allows the trip between these two cities to be completed in approximately 90 minutes, this highway was not completed until the year I was born (1975), making the trip between the cities a very difficult one. In addition, at that time, long distance calls were extremely expensive, making it burdensome to communicate with those in different cities.

My parents and siblings moved to San Juan, and I was born there. That was the first immigration my family experienced. Although 75 miles might not seem like much, the distance from our extended family was a hard challenge for our nuclear family. My parents had to manage parenting and adapting to the capital city without the immediate support of their family. Opportunely, a second family emerged, the church. The Christian church became an essential source of emotional support for my parents. We were part of the same church for most of my childhood and adolescence. I have fond memories of the people there, as these individuals became like family to us.

My Early Childhood

I have tender memories of my family's reunions. The extended family would seek opportunities to gather and be together. The women would be in the kitchen preparing elaborate meals while they shared their views of life. The men would discuss politics or share jokes. The children would either play outside or *quietly* join the adults, as children were not supposed to talk when adults were having discussions due to the respect given to elders. Then we would all come together to enjoy the *pasteles, arroz con gandules, pernil,* or the Puerto Rican dish for the day, before ultimately saying our sad goodbyes. These meetings were important in the tradition formation of the children, as they were a venue for exchanging values and beliefs that would guide them in the future.

As early as I can remember, I had been praised—frankly—just for having a penis. I do not think I even knew how to tie my shoes when my family was already celebrating the endless number of girlfriends I would have in the future. Even before being in school, I learned at least two clear lessons:

1. that having a penis gave me power;
2. that I had been granted permission to be promiscuous, of course in heterosexual relationships only.

I also learned that my goal in life was to find a good wife to marry, have children, to provide, and to protect the family. Very early on, I also learned that real men are tough, don't cry, take risks, and often use force to express their power. With that knowledge, I was then equipped to start attending school.

But I was different. I knew I was drawn to boys from a very early age. I have vivid memories of holding hands with other boys and wanting to kiss them. Teachers would scold and publicly ridicule me for insisting on doing that. It did not take me long to learn that this innocent instinct was considered to be disgusting and repulsive by others, especially adults. Much like when Adam and Eve realized they were naked for the first time, I felt shame and a need to cover and hide myself.

My attraction to boys was easier to hide than my mannerism. By the time I was six years old, I must have been a very effeminate boy. I have endless memories of others around me telling me not to talk, walk, or act "that way." According to others, my tone of voice was too high, my wrist was too flexible, and I was too delicate. I was heartbroken to find out that others disliked me and thought of me as defective. I tried very hard to "act more like a man," but I didn't seem to be such a good actor as I was often bullied. I often felt scared, crushed with sadness, and helpless. The embarrassment of not being "man enough" to defend myself or to stop my *sissyness* prevented me from reaching out or telling anyone. I was alone and had no support to face this.

Even though I struggled with my mannerism and my attraction to boys during my childhood, I did not think of myself as gay. At that time, I did not know, nor did I understand, what sexual orientation was. However, I was taught to hate gays that early. By age seven, I already had heard multiple sermons about the sinfulness and abomination of homosexuality. I knew about Sodom and Gomorrah, before I knew how babies were made or what rape was. I heard several times how God hated gays because they were weak, led by vice, and were an abomination. These lessons were accompanied by details on how terrible and painful hell was; the smell, the heat, the noise, and the constant agony of that place. Those lessons made it clear that homosexuals would rot or burn (or maybe both) in hell. Even though I had no idea what being gay was, I was sure I hated gays too and that I did not want to be even close to anyone like that.

Stories and songs were common ways used by the church to teach their lessons to children. A song I remember very well went like this: "Cuidadito, cuidadito lo que haces . . . por que hay un Dios de amor que mirandote esta . . . Cuidadito con lo que haces." Basically, the song states that there is a God of love who is always watching us, so we'd better be careful what we do. I don't know if it was the contagious cheery melody, but this message stuck with me. I felt watched and judged all the time. Then again, behaviors are easier to control than feelings and thoughts. I could control how I acted, and deny my attraction to other boys, but I couldn't control the feelings I had inside. The thought of God being able to know my thoughts and feelings kept me continuously nervous and uneasy. This became a constant battle. Most nights I would pray for God to change me, feeling like I had a stake through my heart, in agony, crying until I fell asleep. All I wanted was to please God and my family, and I was disgusted by my nature.

Not all my early education about homosexuality came from the church. In the absence of real role models or formal education about homosexuality, television became a clear influence that shaped my thoughts about it. Extreme stereotypes were consistently portrayed, with the message that gay people deserved to be ridiculed and hated. Gay men were portrayed as less than "real men," and as though they often wanted to be women. The overall message was one of devaluation, rejection, and hatred. As a result, I internalized these messages. I believed them as true. It is a difficult thing to learn that who you are is hated with such devotion by others. A bitter memory that often comes to mind is the funeral of Matthew Shepard, a young gay man who was brutally murdered in an anti-gay hate crime in Wyoming in October 1998, where some religious groups held signs stating things like "God hates Fags!" Such messages were so consistent and prominent that at that time my solution was to avoid being myself at all costs.

I tried to be "good," to fit in, and to earn the approval of others, especially my family. On one side there was a life of sin, dishonor, and sickness leading to hell. On the other, I got to keep my family and friends; I would be respected, have a family of my own, and the possibility of going to heaven. I did all I could to gain their approval. I had great grades, was responsible and well behaved. I also attempted to suppress any thoughts or feelings connected to my homosexuality. Along with those suppressed feelings, I also suppressed my self-interest and individuality.

No matter what I did, it didn't wash away who I was. None of my efforts achieved the eradication of the homosexual in me. It is hard to grow up not knowing if the people you love would love the real you. It is hard to grow up believing that there are conditions to being loved. Sure, my parents expressed a lot of love to the "good" me, and they were always proud of my achievements.

But I would ask myself, "If they knew the truth inside, would they still love me?" Other questions followed in circles without resolution: "How could I even consider disrespecting my family and my God? Would the pain destroy my family? Could I handle true isolation? Could I handle being a single digit, outside a unit?"

Many people cherish their childhood memories and wish they could go back to such a good time in their life. I do not feel that way. My childhood was very painful. No adult ever reached out to tell me it was okay to be me. To pretend to be something you are not, just because others want you to be that, is exhausting. Constant pretending led me to more silence and eventually to a deep loneliness. I remember times in school where I did not know where to go or what to do. I was so lonely and disconnected that I had no place. There were times that I would lock myself in the bathroom, waiting for the lunch hour to pass. My mother noticed my isolation and was concerned. She made great efforts to get me to interact with other children. She even had me play every sport there was, but I did not do well in any of them, nor seem to make friends. Actually, at times it seemed that the opposite occurred; the more exposed I was to others, the less liked I felt.

Not surprisingly, I felt alone in the world, hiding in a place much deeper than a closet. No one in the world knew the real me. Not even me. There was a point in my childhood where I learned how to dissociate and be surrounded by people but not *be there*. Exploring my homosexual feelings and expressing what I felt was not an option. It was not a choice to lose my family. It was not a choice to disrespect my family or my religion. It was not a choice to feel like I felt. It was not a choice to act like I would have normally acted. Therefore, I was a void, almost like a robot, with no emotions and relying on others for a program to tell me how to act and what to express.

Puberty Is Here

As I reached puberty somehow things got a bit easier. My body started to change and that was a good thing. At age 12, I had become one of the tallest, my voice became deeper, my skin a bit rougher, and I developed facial hair. All of a sudden my soft boyish look was "blessed" by nature with a "rough" adolescent look. I told myself, "What a relief, I am less obviously gay." Acting like "a man" became easier and more believable. This granted me access to certain privilege. Once I was able to occasionally "pass for straight," I could have some of the benefits of being part of society. Almost overnight, people felt less threatened by me, and I started getting friends. It felt good to be part of a group, but to keep their acceptance I told myself, "I cannot be my true self." Moreover, in order to emphasize that I was not gay, I had to demonstrate it by degrading, making fun of, and rejecting anyone else who might raise suspicion that they were that way.

Intense attractions came along with puberty. I tried to convince myself that I was attracted to the same girls that my friends were. Cognitively, I was able to achieve that, but in reality my glances and emotions would unconsciously center on boys in ways that made others around me uncomfortable. As a result, I was part of groups, but I was never fully integrated or trusted.

Among the developmental tasks adolescents face are developing abstract thinking, identifying meaningful moral standards, getting along with others, adjusting to a sexually maturing body and feelings, preparing for a job or career, and becoming more self-sufficient while establishing key aspects of identity. All of these were challenged due to my sexual orientation. Being gay does not affect the development of cognitive, emotional, moral, or social skills; however, living in a homophobic, heterosexist, and sexist society does. The simple task of "thinking" is harder when your mind is struggling to make sense of the inconsistency between your inner world and the opposite messages experienced on a daily basis. Becoming self-sufficient was also a challenge, given that I had denied myself the right to be me.

It was confusing to confront a maturing body and feel attractions when my sexuality was to be invisible. It was challenging to build a proud identity when I could not openly explore who I was. Therefore, my focus became to prepare for my future career. Early in my life, I recognized intellectual ability as my strength and my passport to the future. Since my adolescence, I was sure I would go to college and complete a doctorate.

Just before going to college, my father got into a very heated argument with both of my siblings. In an attempt to stop the altercation I screamed, "At least you have children, I will never have children!" I thought it was a vague and indirect statement but it was not. The argument stopped. A few minutes later my father approached me and asked what I meant by the comment. All I responded was that I wanted to see a psychologist.

The first day with the psychologist, I told her that I thought I had gay tendencies, and I wanted to change this. With an empathic face she looked at me and told me that she could not help me do this. She told me she could not change sexual orientation in a person, nor would she want to do so. She continued by stating that if I allowed her time for us to meet, we could discuss why changing my sexual orientation was important for me, and in the process we could also explore what alternatives I had to find happiness in my life. At that time, I am not sure how much I really heard, as I immediately was thinking about how to find another psychologist who changed sexual orientations because this psychologist was no good. But I gave her a try. I did meet with her for about a year. During the first few sessions, I felt irritated, because all she did was normalize homosexuality and I just did not agree with her. She felt it was natural and okay to be gay. She did not think it was a sin or that it was disgusting. As time passed, I started questioning all that societal oppression and moved toward accepting the possibility of allowing myself to be "me," inside and outside. My healing process started here.[2]

Off to the University, Five Miles Away

For my undergraduate degree I went to the University of Puerto Rico, five miles away from home. Attending the university was a blessing for me, mainly because I met people who were interested in pulling out and celebrating the "me" behind the mask. I have no words to describe how special Yerica, my college friend, was. One day, she looked at me and said, "Héctor, I know you and who you are inside, and I love you more because of it. I hope soon you can love yourself too, just as you are. I also hope the world can see it too." She was the first person I ever told

I was gay. Jorge was the second. Meeting another gay young man with a religious background for the first time was life changing. The two of them nurtured and helped me love myself, and I felt like my life just began then. For the first time, I liked who I was. As the ugly duckling, I found the pond with swans, and I understood that all along it wasn't that I was an ugly duckling, but that I was different from those around me. Acknowledging my sexual orientation and not denying it did not mean that I automatically accepted it or that I was able to proudly celebrate who I was. But these friends at college accelerated my process of building a strong and healthy sexual identity. In my last year of undergraduate schooling, my friends encouraged me to take a course on LGBT psychology. It was then that I met Dr. Joe Toro-Alfonso, my first real role model. His course and life work inspire me still today. Taking this class shaped my life and led me to a career with a focus on working with LGBT individuals.

Moving to the USA

For some time, I felt like I was living a double life, "straight" with my family and gay elsewhere, as many Latino gay men feel. This double life was a distortion of reality, and led me to feel shame for lying and deceiving my family. As I became more openly gay and an LGBT advocate, I felt the need to live a more honest life. I knew it would hurt my family, but hiding who I was would not change who I was. The opportunity to immigrate to the US came and I followed it in the hopes of finding the freedom to express my sexuality. Now I understand that the decision to move in part was due to my own internalized homophobia, leading me to feel the need to escape and hide. I still had not fully accepted myself at that time, and although I was somewhat comfortable with my sexual orientation, I was not comfortable being completely open about it and accepting the vulnerabilities that would expose me. Ironically, I moved to express my gayness more openly, but in actuality I was hiding. I moved to protect my family from the pain of having a gay family member, but I might have hurt them more by preventing them from having me nearby and developing a deeper relationship with me. I never told them the reason for my move. I just packed a bag and left within a month of making the decision.

Before moving to the US, it did not cross my mind that I would face ethnic and racial oppression. Race granted certain privileges, which I was unaware of until I lost them. In the US, I experienced both advantages due to my race (being light skinned "for a Puerto Rican") and disadvantages due to my ethnicity, language difficulties, and origin. These experiences challenged me and led me to move from a state where I was "color blind" and did not understand the significance of race as an issue, to a place where I better understood privilege and racism, and I was making genuine attempts to be antiracist and address social injustice.[3]

While living in the US, I continued working to accept and develop pride in my sexual identity. I started integrating these two identities. In the meantime, my issues of masculinity continued. I pondered over the expectations of a stereotypical heterosexual man and the stereotypical gay man, in an attempt to find myself reflected in one of those two. I wanted to let go of the limited definition of being a man society had fed me, but I still found myself engaging in sexist and gender biased behaviors. For example, in my relationships I would push myself to always be stoic and in control as I was the "man." From accepting and complying with society's expectations of me as a man, I moved to a place where I started to question society's limiting demands. Multiple unsuccessful attempts to develop meaningful romantic relationships due to my inability to connect and be vulnerable led me to question my issues of masculinity more seriously. At that time, I did not know how much effort it was going to take to be ready to honestly love another man and truly establish a committed relationship. The opportunity to take the next step in this hard journey of transformation and letting go of oppressive sexist notions came along nine years ago, when I met Mike, my lifelong partner. Finding a person of worth to build my life with forced me to also build necessary skills to successfully maintain a relationship and the challenges that accompany that. These challenges included having only hetero-sexual relationships as a guide from which to build my own relationships, negotiating traditional male roles within a relationship between two men, facing communication challenges and difficulty expressing emotions, having difficulty with my feelings of competitiveness, feeling the urge to always be strong and the inability to be vulnerable, and, finally, not knowing how to experience anger without exploding, running away, or escaping.

What is more, in the process I learned that part of the hate toward homosexuality is related to issues of masculinity and sexism. We live in a society that values males over females. Society has led us to believe that masculinity and femininity are at the two opposing ends of the spectrum. Therefore, there is an unspoken rule which states that a man who is not "manly" or does not demonstrate stereotypical characteristics of the masculinity hegemony is worth less. Characteristics such as "weakness," "softness," and "emotionality" have been assigned as stereotypical characteristics of women, and as a general rule men tend to reject and avoid any behavior that may be assigned to women. Such a restricted definition of masculinity is problematic as it excludes many legitimate expressions of masculinity and pressures men to restrict their behavior to a limited notion of what it is to be masculine. Also, such a limited definition leads to an intolerance of vulnerability and a constant need for males to demonstrate and prove their masculinity to others.

As I became older, I realized not only that this pressure was imposed on me as a gay man, but that most men feel this pressure to demonstrate and prove their masculinity. An attractive woman walks by and this becomes an opportunity for some men to demonstrate their heterosexuality and masculinity. They may shout sexist offensive remarks, which may not really be intended for the woman but for the audience that acknowledges this as an act of virility. Men may choose to select people in their private lives with whom they don't need to guard their masculinity, but in most social situations the shield goes up and there is a pressure to perform. Combined with a lack of coping mechanisms, this need to demonstrate masculinity can lead to the regrettable use of violence, even toward those we love. I have never been physically violent, but I have used other forms of violence to impose my masculinity on others. I regret having used negative nonverbal behavior, indirect intimidation, competitiveness, deprivation, and other controlling behaviors as a way to publicize my fragile masculinity. As I have moved toward an active awareness state of my own masculinity, I have become more comfortable where I stand and feel no need to convince others about how much of a man I am.

Conclusion

I can now reflect on how proud I am of where I come from, what I have achieved, and who I have become. Memories cannot be undone, and I wish I could go back and embrace that little boy and tell him he was perfect just as he was. I want to tell him that no matter if he bent his wrist, spoke softly, acted effeminately, embraced other boys, or loved other boys, I would love him unconditionally. At the same time, I feel very fortunate, because even though at times I felt extremely lonely and disconnected from my family, they were always there and loved me deeply. I often wonder what would have become of me without all the protective factors on my side. Without a caring family, parents who instilled positive values in me, a comfortable socioeconomic status, living in a safe neighborhood, having light skin, having a strong sense of spirituality, having mentors and people who care about me, where would I be? Would I have survived? Today I am close to my nuclear family, I have a family of my own, and I feel connected to my spiritual beliefs, all of which provides me great support. There is a lot I still have to learn in this life, but because of their love and support I feel confident I will be okay as my life continues to unfold.

BILL'S STORY

Benign Beginnings

Elkhorn, in southeastern Wisconsin, was a White boy's paradise. It was a small town, it was a safe town, and I didn't have to worry about a thing.

I remember summertime best; I would eat my breakfast, meet my neighborhood chums in the driveway, and off we would go on our bikes for the rest of the day. It was a time when parents didn't worry about the whereabouts of their children—my stay-at-home mom knew I would be safe because I had a whole community watching out for me. And I had a sense of that too.

My friends and I weren't exactly doing safe things—playing on the south end of town at the fuel farm, on the railroad tracks, and in the abandoned factory. But we always knew that somebody would help us if we needed it. Elkhorn worked just fine for me. I was protected and insulated from bad things.

Maybe I heard about them from my other elementary school-age cronies—urban legends about kids who found themselves in unlikely peril in haunted houses or at the hands of crazed child snatchers—but that didn't happen to anyone we actually knew. We just liked to impress each other with those stories, handed down to us by older siblings or older kids in the neighborhood—sworn to as "the God's honest truth." And then there were those occasional snippets from the nightly news that described a war in a faraway land—body counts, KIAs, and MIAs—combat reporters talking to us from muddy rice paddies as we sat at the table eating our dinner.

I lived in the quintessential American mainstream nuclear family—a mother, a father, a brother, and a dog. My parents' roles were highly delineated, stable and traditional: my father provided for us by working outside the home, while my mother managed all aspects of the household and of child-rearing, proud to be known as a "homemaker." It was my mother who was responsible for that critical nurturing of young children—and she was very good at it. I do not remember in those early days feeling any sense of uncertainty, lack of love, or lack of physical or emotional comforting.

America was set up for us and by us. We could go anywhere, at any time, with anyone we pleased. There were no borders—physical or racial. Our family politics were conservative, which when I look back on it makes sense. Why support change when the status quo was so good to us?

My father was a very hard working man, an attorney with a reputation for honesty and integrity. Our family name was revered in Elkhorn, my grandfather having been a popular mayor who died in office when my father was still in high school—thereby cementing his legacy as a good leader. We were upper middle class, and we were upwardly mobile. I really wasn't even aware of things like family names and reputations; I was just a carefree kid—fully enjoying the innocence of childhood. I didn't really notice that my father worked a lot—I just thought that was what men did. To this day, I can still remember his work schedule: Monday through Friday at the office or courthouse all day with a break for lunch and a break for dinner, return to the office after dinner until nine or ten o'clock at night, work half a day on Saturday, off on Sunday, and repeat—for years. What I didn't know was that my father was covering for a partner with failing health, doing much of that partner's work as well as his own—keeping up appearances that everything was fine, for the sake of his practice and the families.

My role model father was the epitome of the tough, stoic, self-reliant man. We had fun with my dad—my brother and I; he would throw the football to us out in the yard, he would give us piggy-back rides on his shoulders, we would do yard work together. We never detected any change in his demeanor, his emotional state, or his attitude toward life—only the occasional and brief bout of irritability after work on some nights, but he was quite good at bottling that up. I learned vicariously through him to be that way—to hide stress, sadness, emotion, and fatigue—for my own good and the good of the family. Because that is what men do.

As I grew, I began to learn more about the stresses he was under. His practice did finally dissolve as his partner's difficulties became more pronounced. I also came to know that my father was and had been helping out others in distress financially and otherwise. As I reflect on that now, it was almost like he was the George Bailey of Elkhorn—keeping things moving forward while keeping the secrets of others. He had such a sense of place and personal responsibility for his family and community. So yes, he was tough, stoic, and self-reliant; but he was not a man who desired to climb corporate ladders, acquire more things, and make it known to others that he was doing that. Humility, financial conservatism, and commitment . . . these were also my father's hallmarks.

Boyhood Lost and the Lore of "Others"

Elkhorn was exclusively White. It was about as homogeneous as a community can get. All my friends looked like me, all their families looked like ours, and I had very little experience of racial diversity. I was aware of places like Milwaukee and Chicago, and I had heard others talk about other races and creeds, but this talk was frankly never positive and almost always stereotypical. It wasn't coming from my parents, but it was coming from some of my friends, relatives, and adults in our community. I learned as I aged into my tween years, for example, that Jewish men were called "kikes" and for some reason they couldn't be trusted in business, that Black men were called "niggers" and they should actually be feared, and that Latinos were called "wetbacks" and they were only good for harvesting crops. So became the lore of "others"—those that I had no experience with. I didn't learn how to hate them—the talk wasn't that strident or virulent—but I certainly learned to distrust, avoid, categorize, and to some extent fear.

As I advanced through middle school, the innocence and naiveté of childhood began to give way to attitudes and behaviors that were pseudo-adolescent in nature—comparisons of physical strength and athletic ability, friendships based on social standing, and interest in girls. It was as if a line were being crossed between two ways-of-being. I was slow to cross that line and more or less stumbled across it behind many of my peers. I can remember being ill-prepared for such things as interscholastic athletic competition, somehow making the starting team in basketball but completely choking during our first game, ultimately being benched and replaced permanently in the line-up by one of my best childhood friends. He didn't let me hear the end of it for the rest of the season, and we were never the same in our relationship.

I was a tall but very thin, gawky, allergy-ridden pre-teen who didn't fare all that well on the playground when it came to feats of strength or head-to-head competition with my peers in such things as wrestling or play-fighting. But most disturbing of all, I was shocked to see some of my childhood friends now holding hands with girls at school dances and even slow dancing with them! I was not ready for that sort of transition. Girls mystified and petrified me. If any girl showed interest in me—typically expressed through flowery handwritten notes or third parties—I felt some pride, but mainly panic. I was simply not ready to emerge from childhood yet, where things were much easier and that way-of-being so familiar. In fact, I still preferred to play with my G.I. Joe action figures and Hot Wheels cars, or so many of those outdoor childhood games, over practicing my jump shot or challenging my peers to physical combat or posing in front of the mirror analyzing my appearance.

Yet I *was* starting to feel left behind. It was harder to find same-age friends to do those things with, and I knew it wasn't a good idea to start playing with younger kids. In a way, I was stuck and didn't know how to get myself unstuck. It didn't even occur to me to ask my peers, my teachers, or my parents for help. Maybe it was boyhood social learning that forbade it—asking for help and being vulnerable ran counter to the requirement to be unemotional and self-reliant. I'm not sure anyone around me noticed my inner conflict—I was very good at hiding my emotions. This is a trait my wife, Rebecca, still notices in me to this day.

When I reflect on this period of my life, I think about Pollack's notion (described in Chapter 3) that boys can often be prematurely separated from their psychic nurturing environment, ultimately feeling shame about needing connection and subsequently leaving deficits in the areas of intimacy, empathy, and commitment in relationships as adult men.[4] Or Bergman's notion (also described in Chapter 3) that boys feel pressure to disconnect from themselves in order to achieve in the world—to do things, fix things, and be competent.[5] If those things were true for me, they would have occurred at that time of my life. As I think about it now, I believe I was lonely during those years. I wasn't being ignored by people who could help me; I just wasn't cognitively or emotionally available to benefit from anyone's guidance or advice. And despite the fact that I am now a psychologist, I do at times struggle with intimacy, sharing, and trust. It is sometimes hard to find the words to describe how I feel, or to express strong emotions other than anger. It is a weakness that I must always be aware of and compensate for in all my relationships.

Adolescent Lessons

Ultimately though, that transition did occur for me as I entered high school. Childhood was clearly gone. I was in a completely new game now, with rules for young men that were directly applicable to life as adult men. *Be tough, be stoic, acquire things, and be self-reliant*—these were the goals. My small town high school was a real proving ground for us. I was a student there during the late 1970s, a time in this country when in general adults and parents took a more hands-off approach to childrearing and guidance of young people. And my cohort took full advantage of that. Many kids were already getting drunk, getting high, and experimenting with sex (usually in that order) by the time our freshman year ended. Discipline in the school was lax, and for many of us it felt as if the upper classmen were in charge. When I was required to read *Lord of the Flies* in English Literature, I then understood how to contextualize our experience.

Bullying and intimidation were not fully understood or recognized in that time. It wasn't condoned by our school staff, but it perhaps wasn't viewed as damaging either. There were likely no staff in-services on the topic and no real plan to reduce it. The staff may not have really been aware of its extent either, as much of the activity took place in unsupervised settings and times throughout any given day. But it *was* there and, like any social phenomenon, it became more elaborate and widespread over time. For example, a simple punch to the head was not really that impressive; but several hard punches to the ear until bleeding occurred, all while the teacher was distracted taking attendance and in full view of the entire class—this was clearly recognized as having the "wow" factor. And the bully was unfortunately socially reinforced for the behavior by his peers, which then led to even more of it.

By the way, it was not I who received those blows to the head; but I witnessed it. I can still see the victim's face to this day—he was trying to be stoic and act as if nothing was happening, but also trying to hold back tears. And he endured that treatment regularly for the rest of his high school time. Given that as young men we feel such intense shame when we fail to live up to the accepted masculine ideal, I can't imagine how that kind of treatment affected him and other victims during that important developmental phase of adolescence. In fact, I still feel that intense reaction even as an adult—ruminating about how I *should* have acted when challenged or confronted, and perhaps rewriting history a bit over time to make the actual event more palatable to me.

It may be disappointing or a relief at this point in my story that I report not being victimized all that much in high school—certainly not to the extent described above. During my early years there, I was not truly an outlier or a target—I had re-engaged in sports, I hit puberty so my physique was improving, and I had become known as a chronicler of high school life through my caricatures and drawings of daily occurrences. The social leaders of my class thought these were entertaining, so I had some credibility and hence protection.

Yet I *can* say that I was harassed from time to time (the worst coming during my recovery from knee surgery and having the crutches routinely kicked out from underneath me while trying to navigate stairwells and hallways), that I was also a witness to bullying, and—sadly—I myself was also party to it. Hence, I played all those roles, which research on bullying now confirms as typical for young males. It was that way-of-being again—the need to be perceived as tough, but also popular and accepted by the group. It was this latter goal that certainly drove a lot of my behavior.

It did that, but right up to the point where I eventually decided I'd had enough. And I credit one kid for that—my friend Jack. He didn't start out that way with me. He was a true outlier—interested in soccer before anyone ever played it in America, interested in war/fantasy gaming before anyone ever knew what that was, and just a big gangly guy who was an easy mark for bullying. For a while, I was part of the campaign to make his life miserable, but I was also surreptitiously interested in some of the same things, making a beginning friendship possible. I'm not even sure how that happened, but I do clearly remember a day where I had to make a choice about it. Jack was walking to school ahead of me and several other kids. As per the harassment program for outliers, we started to taunt him, trip him, and throw gravel at him. I quickly became conflicted about it, feeling guilt about what I was doing but not being brave enough to stop it—until Jack turned around and stared right at me, right through me, and no one else. That's all he did, and that's all he had to do for me to realize I needed to stop following the herd.

From that point forward, our friendship grew and I never bullied him again, nor did I assume the cowardly bystander role if someone came after him. I don't think I ever apologized to Jack, but adolescent boys rarely do that without adult pressure. We just had one of those unspoken understandings, evidenced in the way we now interacted—which comes much easier than words for adolescent males. Jack actually became my best friend during our remaining years of high school, and we became somewhat of a mystery to the rest of our class—an odd couple of sorts who began rejecting the high school "system," rejecting pretty much anything mainstream, and ultimately—to the chagrin of our parents—trashing our GPAs to the point where we barely graduated from high school. Along with that rejection came familiarity with alcohol and marijuana (the latter being at its peak in American high schools during that time), delusions of becoming rock stars (with only minimal experience in actually playing instruments), a lot of late-night driving around getting into mischief, and a dedication to not going on to college, which was, I'm sure, a source of huge concern to our parents. But we were just not available to benefit from their advice in the matter, which for me was reminiscent of my hesitancy in middle school to ask for help. It was that boyhood social learning again, this time the adolescent version in which self-reliance meant an active rejection of adult guidance.

Frankly, I can't remember any adults who may have influenced me one way or the other during those years—we were pretty much making it up as we went along. When reflecting on my adolescence now as a psychologist who knows what young men need, I believe I did not feel very *protected*, I do not recall being very *educated* about what I was going through, and I know I was nearly completely dis*connected* from my small town environment. It really was no one's fault, my parents and teachers did the best they could in trying to understand a rapidly changing social environment for teenagers. It was a time when just about everyone—adults included—seemed to be struggling to find their way again in that difficult post-Vietnam, post-Watergate environment.

Yet perhaps because of that small town setting, and a comforting background feeling that my parents still cared about me, and the grace of God—I did not descend into more serious trouble, despite two years of drifting beyond high school. Shockingly, I did not become a rock star (although I continue to enjoy playing guitar to this day), and I found out after two years how limited my upward mobility was going to be with a high school degree. I think it was third shift work in a ceiling tile factory that finally drove me back into educational pursuits—that and the feeling I was being left behind again, just like in middle school. This time I had awareness—I knew I needed to take that developmental step consciously, rather than stumble through it.

Young, White, and Male: Privilege and Protection

So off to the University of Wisconsin-Milwaukee I went. Like so many others on campus, I was not sure why I was there. I just knew it was a better place than where I had been. But over time I began to hone my interests, take education much more seriously (working on degrees in political science and history), and became open to new ways of thinking about things. But not too much—for despite the fact that the city of Milwaukee's population was predominantly minority, the university was not. Hence, I continued to think of people who were unlike me as "others," not in a hateful sense but in an avoidant one. My group of similar-looking friends reinforced this notion of separation and, frankly, superiority over not only minorities of all kinds (including sexual) but also women.

Yes, we engaged in the usual college partying, drinking, clubbing, and scoring—or at least attempts to do the latter. I had been in only one dating relationship in my life thus far. Girls still made me uneasy—they were difficult to understand and please, but admittedly very nice to look at and ultimately pursue. I learned from my more experienced guy friends how to do this, although this learning was clearly skewed in the direction of acquisition and conquest. So, once again, as a young man I was subject to those masculinity directives of toughness, stoicism, lack of relational commitment, and acquisition based on one's own effort. I was just plodding along, unaware of or unwilling to consider alternative ways of being a man, accepting conventional notions of masculinity, endorsing restrictive views of gender, and very dependent on reinforcement by my peers.

At the same time, as my adolescent rebelliousness started settling down, I became more conservative and more accepting of my White middle-American identity. And as my undergraduate years ended, I started looking to the military—because that was a tradition for the men in my family; my grandfather, my father, and all my uncles. I began to view this as my next step because it fit so well with who I was becoming and who I thought I should be. Again, the ideal of masculinity related to toughness, competence, achievement, and pride was clearly evident in my thinking—but that is in hindsight. At the time, I really felt the need to just demonstrate all of these things. Image and respect are everything for a young man—and in that way, a man in uniform is hard to beat.

I chose the navy, mainly because my father had and he always spoke highly of that time. I remember listening to his stories of the Naval Academy, being on a battleship, and sailing to places like North Africa and the Caribbean. It sounded exciting and exotic. And my timing couldn't have been better. I reported to Aviation Officer Candidate School in Pensacola on the heels of the mega-hit film *An Officer and a Gentleman*, which glamorized the very school I was attending. Soon after that, I reported to Naval Air Station Miramar in San Diego just as the mother of all military mega-hits was released, the ubiquitous *Top Gun*, which was filmed at the base and which also glamorized my chosen profession, naval aviation. It was the late 1980s by then and my status as a military man could not have been higher. My fellow flyers and I were treated by virtually everyone in the country as American royalty. We could do no wrong, we were all debonair gentlemen warriors who risked our lives at sea flying off aircraft carriers, holding the communist hordes at bay, protecting our American way of life. The Officer's Club at Miramar became *the* destination for women who were looking for that glamorized man—and it was packed almost every night.

So, if I was seeking respect and trying to craft an image of heroism and ruggedness for myself, I had achieved it—really through no significant effort on my part. It was hard—very hard—not to believe our own glamorized press, particularly when no one was whispering words of restraint in the other ear. There were two things happening simultaneously during those years. The first was an endless validation of my masculinity through an almost totally male-dominated way of life. Being on an aircraft carrier with thousands of other like-minded men, literally cut off from a more balanced view of the world, produced a way of looking at others—even the citizens we were tasked to protect—that was inferiority based. To many of us, the places we visited were inhabited by substandard people—like "flips," "gooks," and "ragheads."

The second thing happening was actually more positive. An aircraft carrier was like a floating city—roughly six to eight thousand men aboard. And there was certainly diversity among that population. In fact, I believe that virtually every race and socioeconomic class was represented in a ship that big. We did have to tolerate each other in very cramped quarters, in very uncomfortable conditions, and for long periods of time (six to eight months each cruise). And I did begin to learn more about my fellow man through this experience, despite the fact that, as an officer, I was part of a largely White contingent of men who told other men—many of whom were minorities—what to do. And we didn't have to be that polite about it.

Nevertheless, I was able to catch a glimpse of what life for non-White men was really like. That glimpse, combined with the experience of other cultures in faraway places (much of it quite desperate), started to stir something inside of me that superseded my jingoistic view of others. Mind you, I was still full of myself; but I was thankfully just intelligent and reflective enough to begin to see the other side of the male coin. That's the side that we don't like to show anyone or even acknowledge exists. It is that side of us that is perhaps more sensitive, pensive, vulnerable, and desiring of connection. That trend in me continued for a few more years, until I ultimately decided to act on it and left the navy. I wasn't quite sure what I was going to do; I only knew that I needed to move on.

Enlightenment Dawns

I was in my thirties, alone, and without a career; but for perhaps the first time in my life I was becoming aware of my biases and privilege. Enough variables that had been acting on me in a negative way—arresting my development as a man—started flipping to the positive, and the possibility of moving forward was there for me. I moved back home, to Madison this time and to the University of Wisconsin. I took some classes; I became interested in psychology, and the rest, as they say . . .

Am I now a better man than I was? Have I consciously transformed the way I view my masculinity to the point where I am now actively aware? Probably not; I still make my mistakes, I misperceive that I am more important as a White man than I really am. I probably commit flagrant micro-aggressions toward my colleagues Héctor and Ramel on a regular basis without being aware of it. But I can safely say that now, for the first time in my life, I am in relationship with these "others," on a very personal level. We are equals and we disagree about much; but we also find those areas that we do agree on, and make that the focus of our work. It is this process that we believe will ultimately make our society more peaceful and verdant; so we simply try to model it every time people watch us do what we do.

And as for being alone, I have been granted by God undeserved gifts: my wonderful wife, Rebecca, and our two daughters. Rebecca and I met and fell in love as I was finishing my time in graduate school, readying myself to re-enter the workforce. She taught me to acknowledge and value my very human need for connection and to be vulnerable—to bring those things forward in my life as a changed man. And in the present, she and my daughters all lovingly help keep me humble, centered, and enlightened about what really matters in life. And I thank them from the bottom of my heart for that.

RAMEL'S STORY

When Life Is Not a Crystal Stair

A young man matriculates through manhood as a person walking up an extreme set of stairs. Some journeys are effortless; it appears some are riding on escalators. However, for far too many of our sons, those stairs are steep and filled with tacks, splinters and boards turned up with no carpet to cover the floors— just bare. Despite these odds many boys still move into manhood, but not without consequences.

Frederick Douglas stated that "it is easier to build strong boys than to repair broken men." Sigmund Freud, credited as being the father of modern psychology, understood this point and emphasized how the early stages of life heavily impacted our lives as adults. The Centers for Disease Control and Prevention collaborated with Kaiser Permanente's Health Appraisal Clinic to help determine the link between adverse childhood effects (e.g., physical, sexual, emotional abuse and other familial dysfunctions) and later effects on one's mental and physical health and overall quality of life.[6] This robust study verified, in frightening fashion, that both men and women who experience multiple childhood traumas are at risk for an earlier death and overall lower quality of life. The lower quality of life is attributed to the counterproductive coping mechanisms used to disassociate from the early trauma. Sadly, the socialization of men in western society teaches, almost requires us to lean toward destructive patterns to cope with pain. Young men are covertly, and sometimes overtly, encouraged to hide their emotions or to express them in an aggressive and violent fashion so as not to risk ridicule for behavior unworthy of manhood status. The key is to understand that there is a problem now—and, with this knowledge, reflect back on our past and recognize our past hurts and our past destructive patterns in order to build a better present and conclusion to the chapter of our life.

Indoctrination

My father told me that when I was born, it was one of the happiest days of his life. He was so excited that he gave away the celebratory cigars and vowed he would protect me. In the mini-series *Roots* there was a scene in which Kunta Kinte takes his newborn daughter outside and holds her under the stars and states: *"Behold the only thing greater than yourself."* Well, my dad performed this same ritual with me. I can never remember a time that he did not encourage me or instill in me the confidence that I could achieve anything I wanted to achieve in this world. I was taught the importance of spirituality, family, education, and love. I was given many words of wisdom from family, friends, and community members throughout the years. There are three pillars that I have used as a foundation to help set the parameters of how I live my life. My mother told me, "Nobody is better than you and you ain't no better than anybody else." My father told me, "It only takes a second to ruin your life." My maternal grandmother told me that "the best way to heal yourself is to help others."

Protect and Provide

As a young boy, I was trained in a warrior-like fashion that easily fit the tradition of African ancestry and American culture. I was told, *"boys don't cry," "if somebody hits you, hit them back right away," "boys don't hit girls," "always look out for your family," "your word is your bond," "if you start something, you finish it," "respect your elders," "always try your best," "family always sticks together,"* and other similar axioms that have survived the test of time due to their social relevance.

However, using these axioms is not as easy as just mechanically imparting and reciting them. The concept of social learning teaches us that individuals learn from what they hear, but also from what they witness. When there is a disconnect between what you hear, are taught, and what you see, it creates a state of cognitive dissonance which is exacerbated in a mind that has not yet reached its full level of cognitive maturity.

For example, when I saw my father cry for the first time, I was extremely confused. This did not add up to me. I remember the next time he tried to tell me that boys don't cry. I was waiting to bring this encounter back to his memory. When he recited this axiom to me, I said, "Then why did you cry at Granddaddy's funeral?" Now, this was a wonderful opportunity to explain that men do cry and it is okay at certain times; yet, he merely told me that some paper got into his eye. At this point, I was convinced that men were not to cry—under any circumstance. And, in the event I did cry, I had to redeem myself with an outrageous violent act to validate my maleness, or offer an asinine excuse.

My parents both came from families with five children and all of them were married with children. I was afforded an opportunity to see male role models who took care of the family's emotional and financial needs. This planted a positive seed in my life about marriage and the importance of family. However, through the years I would see half of these marriages prematurely dissolve, including that of my parents. As an eight-year-old male, I had a difficult time understanding the different nuisances of romantic relationships and could not understand why the family structure was so fragile. Who would protect and provide for us? As a young boy who was taught not to cry, I expressed my anger over the premature break-up of my family through aggression.

It Only Takes a Second

Although my father was not in the home anymore, I can say I have great respect for him because he did not stop being a father. He was not there on a daily basis, but he managed to keep our connection close through regular nightly calls and weekend visits. When there was a problem at school with me, my mother and he could communicate on how to correct it. As a child, I did not consider the myriad of issues that could present with parents that were divorced. However, as I got older I came to understand they had a common fear that allowed them to form this alliance. Later in life, my mother informed me that my father's best friend had told her to watch out for me and my temper. He said he had seen that same temper in my father's youngest brother. All my life, I had heard I was like this uncle, but I thought it was a compliment. He was intelligent, artistic, mechanically inclined, and a nice guy.

My father explained to me one day that he was worried about my temper. Again, this created a dissonance because I thought he wanted me to be tough and to beat people up. In fact, when I fought he would be more concerned if I won than why I had fought in the first place. My father was a very meek man, but my uncles and cousins were hyper-aggressive and those were the men whom I sought to emulate. When my father sought to explain to me the dangers of my temper, I politely ignored his comments. He knew I ignored them, but he kept drilling one statement inside my head: "it only takes one second to ruin your life." Then one day he explained to me why we had to travel so far to see my uncle. He explained to me why everyone was wearing the same clothes in his building. He explained to me why we could not go to other areas of his building. He explained to me why there was so much security. He explained to me why he could never come home with us. He explained to me why he could never come visit us. And then he posed a question to me that hit like a ton of bricks: "Do you want your mom and sister to have to come visit you one day in that same penitentiary?" As a six year old, I vividly remember this statement and it has stuck with me to this very day. It did not change me immediately, but it did make me aware of the dangers of aggressive behavior.

However, it also taught me that I was just like my uncle. When we understand the power of words and self-fulfilling prophecies, parents must be careful about what they say and then be careful that it is properly understood by the child. My uncle was in prison. In my six-year-old mind I assumed that meant I would also be in prison one day. My parents allowed me to have multiple athletic outlets to release my frustration, but in the neighborhoods where I grew up, violence was as common as the ice cream truck. Growing up, I was always one of the smallest and this mandated that I also be one of the toughest, lest I be subjected to constant verbal and physical abuse from the other children. My violent behavior seemed to follow me at home, school, community centers, and even church. There was not a place where I would not fight when I felt I was being disrespected. This is not to say I won every fight, but there was not a challenge I was afraid to accept.

In the second grade, I had a fight with another student who was significantly larger than me. After our fight, he had a great respect for me, and that actually is what began a lifelong friendship. In that time, we fought with our hands and not lethal weapons. I learned through this encounter that violence was a way to win respect. While in the fifth grade, there was a boy who had been held back twice and was upset with me. He wanted to fight me and I could not back down. This fight had a bittersweet ending for me: I did get my "props" from the other children who were afraid of this bully, but I would be less than honest if I did not say he got the best of me in this fight. And this incident was reported to the office, which meant my mother was informed. I was afraid I would be in trouble again for my continuous behavior problems, but my mother had a twist for me. She informed me that my sister would be accompanying me to school the next day to help me handle the situation. When my sister came to the school, she was amazed at the size of this fifth grader, but she put a special fear into this kid and I did not have another problem with him the rest of the year. Now, my sister never had to throw a punch, but she came up there knowing she might have to "put the paws" on this young boy if he did not listen to her warnings. Luckily for him, he did not attempt to engage her physically, because my sister was not the typical girl and was notorious in the neighborhood for her pugilistic prowess. The message of "might makes right" was constantly being reinforced.

In middle school, before the end of my first year, I was in so many fights that I was threatened with expulsion if I was involved in another altercation. The message of my father and his repeated lessons about anger management seemed of little value because I was seemingly always surrounded by chaos. The unwritten code was to always handle your business yourself, without any help or assistance from authority figures. Those who sought out help in a conventional fashion were labeled as a "punk," "fag," "sissy," "snitch," "coward," or a "mark." Anybody in this category could not "roll" with the first team because they could not be trusted to have your back or not to snitch. Reputations among peers were extremely important, and, to earn a name of honor, I was willing to defy the rules of any authority figures, even my parents.

A turning point in my life came when I began to regularly attend church services. The new values to which I was being exposed had a deep impact on my life. My goal was to be more loving and less angry. However, one night after choir rehearsal as I walked out of the stands, someone hit me from behind. Now the hit was not one of great force, but it was one of great disrespect. As the new guy, who was smaller than his peers, even a supposedly docile church boy wanted to test me. He should not have done that. One of the common features of my anger is that I would dissociate during my fights; when they were over, people would explain things to me that I did not even know I did. In this encounter, I recall the first combination I hit him with, and then I just remember three men holding me and telling me to calm down and that "You won." When I looked across the corner, I saw the other young boy with a busted eye and bloody nose crying and saying I had attacked him for no reason.

I was kicked out of the choir and I had embarrassed my maternal grandmother who had been a member of this congregation since its origin. I was told I had to apologize, but I refused because I told them: "I didn't start it, I just finished it." When it came time for us to sing, I just sang that Sunday like nothing happened, almost daring them not to let me sing. That night, my grandmother told me that my anger would not only get me in trouble, but also those who I loved. Then she lovingly asked me to recite the words of the song we had performed that day. She used the hymn to help me understand that my goal was to live the words I sang about, not to be a hypocrite and sing them as empty. This was not the last of my aggressive behavior, but it put me on a path of enlightenment in trying to walk the path of a righteous man. These last two stories illustrate how the women in my life influenced me greatly in my behavior and the road to improvement. And this is why I cringe when I hear the statement, "A woman can't raise a boy to be a man."

A Woman Can't Teach a Boy to Be a Man

There is an old African proverb that states: "It takes a village to raise a child." I do not discount that the role of a positive male role model is absolutely essential in the life of a male child. However, men need to realize that it takes more than one man to raise a child. For example, if I were the only man to raise my sons, they would have all the same flaws and limitations that I have. As a result, I am grateful for the village that is provided for them in the way of extended family, friends, teachers, and community members. My father would always tell me that he wanted me to be a better man than him, and I want the same for my children. Therefore, I want them to be exposed to things I did not have the chance to experience. But I also know that a rooster can still mature if he is raised in a house of hens.

Throughout my life, my mother's words have been a factor that allowed me to walk on an even plane with all other people of different races, SES backgrounds, and other demographics that may have given them an advantage based on the world's standards. A woman cannot raise a man to be a man all alone, but she can help him and raise a good human being. In fact, it was primarily the women in my family that made me the man I would become. I was blessed to see strong women who were educated, classy, fearless, strong, athletic, business savvy, and beautiful. And I later learned that the advice they gave me on how to treat women was much more helpful and beneficial than that of the so-called male experts in my family. The ladies demanded that we treat them with respect. The ladies taught me to be honest, to be chivalrous, transparent, and open. They taught me to treat any prospective lady in my life the way I wanted *them* to be treated. Now, these values may seem old-fashioned and useless for a man trying to play the field, but they are quintessential characteristics for an honorable man. The words of the old James Brown song ring so true, "this is a man's world," but it would not be anything without a woman's touch.

Father Figures

No one can deny that a woman can show a boy how to be a good person and even instruct him on some stereotypically male projects and tasks. However, there are some things that a male needs a male to teach him. I have noticed in my personal and professional life how the certain words of a male figure will often resonate more than those of a female counterpart. Many women bring their sons to me hoping to fill the void left by an absentee father in their sons' lives. These women want desperately to have a positive male role model impart words of wisdom that they cannot provide. As a young man, I was overly blessed to have an abundance of positive male role models in my life that helped to guide me. Ironically I learned that the need for male guidance did not end when I turned 18 or got married or became a father. Even after I had become a licensed psychologist, it was still necessary for me to attach myself to someone who had traveled this path previously.

The men in my family could be categorized as strong, athletic, family-minded, loving, and involved. The absentee father in the Black family is a commonality for far too many of our children, but this concept was foreign to me. Now, the men in my family had another side also, and I think that is what made me respect them even more. None of these men epitomized manhood to me more than my Uncle Charles Freeman. He was tall, strong, could barbeque, was an involved community member, provided for his family, and was known for knocking a sucker out if he got out of line. To me, I always wanted him to be my dad. My Uncle Charles was my senior league baseball coach and he would be tough on me! In fact, he didn't start me my first year on the team. He let me know that everything would be earned.

My parents divorced when I was eight years old. I had two coaches that imparted to me words of wisdom and helped to build my self-esteem using sports as a vehicle to guide me as I navigated through this tough period. Coach Hazelwood and Coach Prince were fine examples of family men who served the community. The next coach to have a strong impact on my life was my high school wrestling coach, Larry West. When I met Coach West, I was at a completely different time in my life. My major problems came from the home setting. At this time, my sister had gone away to college and it was only me and mother in the house together. My mother was working full-time, going to school full-time, and supporting a household alone. Life was filled with tough times and we needed a Dr. Phil or an Iyanla intervention. Well, Coach West would ask me about my life, and after three years of cultivating a relationship from wrestling practices and competitions, I felt comfortable speaking with him about my situation. He would come to my house and hold pseudo-counseling sessions in our kitchen. This was of great significance to me because I was not one of his star wrestlers. I was just a member of his team that he cared for and wanted to help in whatever way possible. Although my mother and I would continue to butt heads throughout high school and college, the time this man took when he had a family of his own left a lasting impression about the importance of men in a young boy's life.

As I matriculated through the halls of high school, I began to search for that rite of passage program that would help me define who I was as a man. I attempted to sign up for the military after graduation; however, I was only seventeen and my mother would not sign the needed adult waiver. Although I was mad at her at the time, this was a turning point because I knew once I was legally emancipated, this would be the last time I would need parental help (at least so I thought). I enrolled in college and I soon understood why Bill Cosby named his college sitcom show, *A Different World*.

Rites of Passage

For all the gains I made in high school, I quickly regressed in college with my thinking about life situations, such as fighting, women, and White people. I graduated from a multicultural high school that was for the college bound. It was not equally diverse, but there was a good mix of students from all racial backgrounds. This mixture allowed us to learn a lot about other cultures and gave us hope that the issue of race could be solved. We were living the manifestation of Martin Luther King's dream. Well, it took me all of about two weeks in Whitewater, WI, to wake up in the nightmare of the real world in my predominantly White undergraduate university.

This university presented me with an opportunity to go through several rites of passage on so many levels. Since the sixth grade, I had been enrolled in schools that were culturally and linguistically diverse; however, in this small college town many of the White students had never interacted with Black students. It was difficult being the only Black person in the class, only because I was treated like the plague by the majority of my classmates. In my first semester, this confused and disturbed me greatly. I quickly learned that the same students who ignored me in class suddenly wanted to be my best friends or turned into the loudest invisible racists after they had been drinking on the weekends. For example, the girls who ignored me in class soon wanted to see if the stereotype of the Black male sexual prowess was true. But others hid behind their dorm room windows and screamed horrible words such as "nigger" and "monkey" and "jungle bunny" so often that I soon began to ignore the comments. If the students weren't bad enough, I would be routinely followed by the police while walking from the library to my dorm. And they weren't following me for protective security. Even more frustrating were the police officers who would confront me with threats of disorderly conduct when I replied back to the racial slurs.

Although I did have some White people I considered positive associates and friends, I saw White people, as a whole, as the White devil. I had not converted to the Nation of Islam, but I began to study more the teachings of the honorable Elijah Muhammad. I began to study more about the true history of this country that is often left outside of the history books. What I read made me even more upset with the people whom I could tell my very presence made nervous.

The campus was estimated to have a school population of about 10,000 students, with about 400 being labeled as African American. The small population of Black students created a safety cocoon for each other, and we embraced this and created a school inside of the school. One of the greatest comforts I found was within my fraternity. Black fraternities are known for their intense pledge programs to gain admittance into the organization. However, what is not known is the amount of positive teaching of knowledge of self, brotherhood, and service to one's community. These were lessons that helped shape my early adult life and still persist in me to this day. The fraternity I pledged was founded on four cardinal principles of Manhood, Scholarship, Perseverance, and Uplift. At the same time as I was lifting these values by promoting social projects at the university, I also espoused a lot of the negative stereotypes. There came a point where I began to lose myself. On any given day, I could be a nerd in the library, in a meeting with the chancellor to increase funding for particular events within the predominantly Black organizations I was associated with, having relations with several women at a time, partying in the University Center, organizing a book drive, or fighting with my team against anybody who challenged us, Black or White.

The day of my graduation, my worst fears were realized. I was arrested. When I went to the courtroom to await my fate—prison, probation, or release— I saw my mother in the courtroom with such a look of disappointment. My lawyer advised me to be quiet because she was sure she could paint a picture of me as a recent college graduate that had served as president of the Gospel Choir and on the executive board for the Black Student Union and my fraternity. She thought she could explain the excessive force used by the police department on the night of the incident. It appeared the case was going my way, because I knew how to play the role of the innocent victim. However, when the judge asked me if I wanted to speak, I told him I did, to my mother's and lawyer's dismay. I described how I was innocent and the victim of a crime by racist cops that had targeted me and people who look like me on a regular basis. Next thing I know, I was given 18 months of probation. My supervision was transferred to Milwaukee, and even my White probation officer laughed at my sentence and stated he thought it appeared too severe. My mother told me if I had kept my mouth shut, I would have been okay and released. I told her I would have rather gone to prison than be that antebellum Negro who was afraid to speak back at master. She told me, "That is why your Kunta Kinte ass is on probation." The night of that arrest was typical of the harassment and brutality young men of color see all too often by the police. I can say without hesitation that *that* night I was not without error, but I was innocent.

The probation was a blessing in disguise because I knew I did not want to go to jail or prison or live my life on probation. I slowly began to try to use the gifts and opportunities I had been given to lead a more productive life. In fact, the words of my grandmother were what rang in my head at this time: "the best way to heal yourself is to help others." To fulfill my community service hours, I went back to the Little League that helped provide a positive direction for me in my youth. I was given the opportunity to instruct young people and I took this seriously. Helping these young men helped me, by giving them a positive role model while reforming myself into a true role model. My success at this job is what made me seriously consider the field of psychology. It did make me feel better to help others and gave me motivation to walk the path of the superior man. I am not proud of all of my past, but I know how every situation has helped me grow and learn and make me the clinician and person that I am today.

You Can Take the Boy out of the Ghetto

In March of 2009, my life changed in a way that still hurts to think about today. After seeing horrific incidents of children being hurt every day and understanding the alarming statistics of children who suffer abuse, I naively thought I could protect my family from these atrocities. I remember receiving a text from my ex-wife stating she needed to talk to me about something. When I returned her call, her first words were, "You know how our daughter be lying?" She then told me that my four-year old daughter had revealed that her boyfriend's 16-year-old son had acted sexually inappropriately toward her. She then followed the statement with: "I'm not sending her to school today because if she tells her teacher this, they will have to report it and he may lose his kids."

When I went to pick up my daughter that Monday night, my ex-wife still had not alerted the authorities about the allegations. Even as I write this story now, I write it with shaking hands, remembering the vivid words that came out of my four-year-old daughter's mouth—how this young man exposed his genitals to her and tried to make her touch his penis. At this time, she demonstrated with her hands how she tried to move his hand, but he kept pulling it back toward the area she was pulling away from. I immediately took her into the police station and filed a report and began the investigation.

After being interviewed by a trained forensic investigator and given a total body examination, it was revealed that there was no structural damage; however, the investigator stated in the police report that "the opinion of the forensic interviewer is that there is a high level of suspicion of sexual abuse." The young man denied all allegations, and his father stated that I coached my daughter to fabricate these allegations. I became more outraged every moment of this investigation. The Assistant District Attorney called me personally and told me that she could not pursue the case because it was not winnable. She stated there were only two people in the room and that my four-year-old girl would have to testify in the court proceedings. Secondly, her mother would testify that her daughter has lied about these types of events in the past. Lastly, she stated that my profession as a psychologist would add credibility to the statement that I had coached my daughter to make these allegations.

After this, my thought process was "fuck the system." My daughter had been abused and neither the system nor her mother had protected her. My first thought was to handle it myself and hurt the boy. My second thought was to hurt the boy. My third thought was to hurt the boy. And if I had seen him at this time, I think

I would have *significantly* hurt him. Any father's worst nightmare is that the women in his life are hurt and violated. Some people hear this and become alarmed that an intelligent, respected, and trained psychologist would even consider vengeance as a tool. Let me try to explain it. When terrorists attacked the World Trade Center in New York City, most Americans wanted immediate retaliation. Well, if a country could feel like this after being attacked, how do you think a father would feel about his first-born daughter?

As time went by, my anger did not dissipate, but I did begin to think in a different way. The court proceedings took months to come to a conclusion. By this time I had observed that my daughter's demeanor had not changed and she seemed to be doing fine. Many men wonder, still, why I didn't hurt him? And the honest answer is that I had felt bad and less-than-a-man because I did not avenge her honor in an aggressive manner. However, what has allowed me to be at peace with my decision are these three reasons: 1) I believe that one reaps what one sows and the young man cannot run from karma; 2) if I had hurt him, I would have gone to prison (prison does not frighten me, but being away from my family does); 3) even if I had hurt him, it would not have removed the abuse she suffered.

No matter what I did, I could not make up for the innocence that had been stolen from her. And the consequences of me hurting him would make her more vulnerable to other predatory attacks that seem consistent with girls who grow up without a father in their lives. My goal now is to make sure I can talk to her and explain the situation, as she is perplexed about why he did it, why he lied and said that he didn't do it, and why he didn't get in trouble for doing it. She also explained how she still likes him and about all of the nice things he had done for her in the past. The fact that I am there to listen to her stories and comfort her when she has night terrors about the situation makes me feel good because I am there to protect her in other ways. My daughter also told me she has forgiven him and that I should, too. Damn, what do you say to that? She does not understand the Stockholm Syndrome or how predators are falsely charming. I told her I would pray on it, but that my level of forgiveness is not as high as hers right now.

I still reserve room for her logic and love, and that it is more elevated than mine on this topic. I began to wonder how I could work with and forgive criminals who had done more devious and nefarious things, but yet I was still holding a grudge when I was personally attacked. I understand from a logical standpoint that forgiving him does not exonerate him, but there is that part of me that wants to see him suffer. Whenever our Building a Better Man trio speak, I often share that I am still a work in progress and I continuously apply our strategies to help improve myself.

As a psychologist, I am trained to help others, but it is just as important that I know how to get myself help in difficult situations. Throughout this process, my entire family has been wonderful and supportive. Though I have experienced a lot of lows, I have been blessed with a beautiful mother and caring sister and extremely supportive extended family that have provided me with a think tank to help resolve personal crises and issues. Further, I have been blessed to have a faithful wife, who has given me four additional children, to help hold me down during those extreme dark moments, and, even more, to provide the simple joys in life that we often take for granted.

These stories about my life presented above are what this book is about. How do we understand ourselves? Are we man enough to grow in ways that are uncomfortable? My goal in writing about a few of the painful experiences in my life is to explain that we also recognize the beautiful parts of life—parts that we take for granted—and learn how to stack on these successes. We must learn from the painful past to help protect our present and fulfill our destiny in the future. As we talk about building a better man, we want to learn and repeat the positives from our past, but also grow and learn from the past experiences of others.

NOTES

1. Falicov, C.J. (1998). *Latino families in therapy: A guide to multicultural practice*. New York: Guilford Press.
2. Cass, V. (1979). Homosexual identity formation: A theoretical model. *Journal of Homosexuality, 4(3)*, 219–235.
3. Helms, J.E. (1995). An update of Helms's White and People of Color racial identity models. In J.G. Ponterotto, J.M. Casas, L.A. Suzuki, & C.M. Alexander (Eds.), *Handbook of multicultural counseling* (pp. 181–198). Thousand Oaks, CA: Sage.
4. Pollack, W.S. (1992). Should men treat women? Dilemmas for the male psychotherapist: Psychoanalytic and developmental perspectives. *Ethics and behavior, 2(1)*, 39–49.
5. Bergman, S.J. (1995). Men's psychological development: A relational perspective. In R. Levant and W. Pollack (Eds.), *A new psychology of men* (pp. 69–90). New York: Basic Books.
6. Felitti, V.J., Anda, R.F., Nordenberg, D., Williamson, D.F., Spitz, A.M., Edwards, V., & Koss, M.P. (1998). The relationship of adult health status to childhood abuse and household dysfunction. *American Journal of Preventive Medicine, 14*, 245–258.

2

ASKING THE RIGHT QUESTIONS IN A VIOLENT SOCIETY

If we do not initiate the young, they will burn down the village to feel the heat.

African proverb

When the three of us began to explore the possibility of working together to promote less violence and encourage better behavior in males, we had to ask ourselves why we believed change was necessary. To us, the answer was simple: "Isn't it obvious?" To our colleagues, particularly within the field of the psychological study of men and masculinity, it may also be. But for others, some convincing may be necessary. So let us examine the lay of the land here in America at the beginning of a new century. Are violence and antisocial behavior really such a big problem?

When discussing a concept as complex as violence, a good place to start is with a definition. In 1996 the World Health Organization (WHO) defined "violence" as: "The intentional use of physical force or power, threatened or actual, against oneself, another person, or against a group or community, that either results in or has a high likelihood of resulting in injury, death, psychological harm, mal development or deprivation."[1] The connotation here is clearly negative, and, for purposes of the following discussion, it is a definition that accurately describes our concern. It is distinct from violence that occurs in the context of controlled and socially acceptable events, such as in athletic competitions (boxing and football). It is also distinct from aggression—or aggressiveness—in humankind's thus far successful battle against the natural conditions of life (e.g., surviving natural disasters or fending off man-eating animals). Arguably, violence can be used positively, as in self-defense or in the defense of others. It can also be used by nation-states in this manner, as in the "just war" scenario. These, however, can be slippery slopes and can lead to misuse and overuse of violence at all levels (e.g., in the legal realm, being charged with excessive use of force in defending oneself; and at the international level, embarking on ill-advised preemptive military action that in hindsight is difficult to justify). The so-called "defensive" or "justified" use of violence is worthy of examination in this regard and is reviewed below.

In the Building a Better Man Project and in our general work as psychologists, we often hear stories of men and boys who were negatively affected by violence as victims, perpetrators, witnesses, or all three. They were in different stages of their lives, differing in age, socioeconomic status, race, and circumstance. What was common about them, however, was an internal sense that they all had to earn their own manhood—that there were certain things they were compelled to think, feel (or not feel), and do in order to be conferred with the title of "a man." Their collective quest to attain that status, whether falling short or succeeding, invariably put them at risk for experiencing violence negatively in one or all three of the roles above.

One should ask if this has always been the case for boys and men, particularly young men. Is it more common now at the beginning of our new century for males to come into contact with violence earlier, more often, and with more lethality? A review of current and historical violence statistics and societal trends suggests that this may be the case. And because more males interact with violence both as perpetrators and as victims, therefore so do more women and children—typically as victims.

In 1999 James Garbarino, in his groundbreaking book *Lost Boys*, reviewed these same statistics and trends and concluded that there was an "epidemic of youth violence" brewing in America.[2] Fifteen years later, it is useful to look again at how these data may have changed. Have the violent youth of the late 1990s become violent adults? Is there still an "epidemic" level of youth violence in a new cohort?

Typically, sociologists and criminologists analyze crime data provided by such sources as the FBI's Uniform Crime Reports (UCR), the Department of Justice's Bureau of Justice Statistics National Crime Victimization Survey (NCVS), and, for juveniles, the Department of Justice's Office of Juvenile Justice and Delinquency Prevention (OJJDP). The Centers for Disease Control (CDC) Division on Violence Prevention also provides data via the National Violent Death Reporting System (NVDRS). The CDC has been involved in violence tracking and prevention since 1980 due to its determination that violence is a serious and ongoing public health threat.

These sources provide annual statistical information about violence in the form of homicide, suicide, aggravated assault, rape, and robbery. Some of these databases track trends in crime back to 1960. Analysis of these trends can be difficult, particularly year to year, and there are many identified confounds to the data that may artificially inflate or deflate these rates both in the short term and long term. However, it does seem clear when viewing the longest-term trends from all data sources that violent crime, including homicide, has actually been decreasing since its peak in the early 1990s. This trend is also consistent for juveniles.[3] Two decades of significantly increasing violence in the 1970s and 1980s seemed to crest at that time. Interpretations of those increases and subsequent decreases are many and are hotly debated in sociology and criminology circles.

So, given Garbarino's assertion that there was an epidemic of youth violence afoot in the late 1990s, if one looks purely at the source data of violent crime to the present, it does not appear that the alleged epidemic lasted—the violent youth of that time did not apparently turn into violent adults. The epidemic does not appear to have spread either—later cohorts of youth have not been as violent since that time.

This news should make us all feel good. We are apparently living in a safer society where we feel more secure, we supervise our children less rigorously, we congregate in large public gatherings without fear or anxiety, and we are all less stressed about the possibility of violence visiting us, our family, or our friends.

But why don't we as a society seem to feel that way?

It may be that statistical crime rates do not tell the whole story when it comes to violence in our society. First, there are the confounds alluded to earlier. For example, trends may be subject to underreporting of incidents (due to the possible illegal activities of victims/witnesses and/or hesitancy to "snitch"), demographic changes (an aging and hence less violent population), improvements in emergency medical care (that keep victims of once-fatal violence alive), and/or increased incarcerations of otherwise violent perpetrators.[4]

The latter is worthy of particular note in that if there are simply more violent men locked up, then yes the violent crime rate may go down. We have the highest incarceration rate in the world, which skyrocketed beginning in the mid-1970s and has not declined since. The United States has 4.46% of the world's population, but represents 22.64% of the world's incarcerated population—much of this due to the War on Drugs, the Three Strikes You're Out rule, and mandatory sentencing.[5] But can we really say that there are numerically fewer violent males in America simply because the violent crime rate has gone down? Prison communities are typically not known for their peace and harmony, despite their "correctional" or "rehabilitation" orientation. In a sense, the problem of violent males may have been shifted from our streets to our correctional facilities. One might even speculate that the violent youth of the late 1990s *did* become violent adults, but they were simply locked up.

Even within the overall trend of decreased violent crime rates in America, there do remain disturbing facts:

- By the end of the twentieth century our society had maintained a level of violence (in terms of reported homicide, assault, rape, and robbery) that was still five times higher than in 1960, when higher-quality crime record-keeping began.[6]

- Rates and trends do not really capture the human toll of violence. Even with a lower homicide rate, there were still an estimated 14,612 reported murders in America in 2011 (roughly 40 people per day). There were also an estimated 751,131 reported aggravated assaults in 2011, the number of victims being sufficient to fill about ten National Football League-type stadiums.[7]

- Disparities in victimization by demography are significant in America. For example, Blacks are far more likely to be victims of homicide than Whites. Overall, young males, minorities, and urban dwellers account for the majority of violent crime victimization.[8]

- Victims of violent crime are not the only ones affected. For every victim, there is a traumatizing effect on other people within that person's family and circle of friends, leading to declines in mental and physical health, and lowered workplace productivity.[9]

- Homicide and suicide are still the second and third, respectively, leading causes of death for 10 to 24 year olds.[10]

- The suicide rate in persons ten years of age and older actually increased for both sexes between 2000 and 2009.[11]

- Compared to Canada and other industrialized countries in Europe, the American homicide rate was generally at the top of the list.[12]

- Current prevalence studies suggest that between 21% and 34% of women will be physically assaulted by an intimate adult partner, while between 14% and 25% of adult women have been raped (up to one out of every four women).[13]

What Garbarino and others who wrote on this subject in the late 1990s were really concerned about was not necessarily the violent crime rate.[14] Actual reported crime can be viewed as the end result of a series of events and circumstances that conspire to produce it. It can be viewed as the mouth of a very long river that has a source, currents, eddies, and rapids. And as an individual floats further downstream, thinking about violence can begin to shift into acting violently, and in that journey a person begins to lose empathy, community, and humanity. This is something obviously less tangible or quantifiable. It is not something the FBI, the Justice Department, or the CDC was evaluating or tracking extensively in 1999. But in the post-Oklahoma City, post-Columbine, and post-9/11 environment, it has become their priority. The central question now is: Who is getting too close to the mouth of the river? Who is nearing that tipping point in which a spillover occurs between contemplation and action?

These writers were not so much concerned about *criminal* behavior as *violent* behavior. It is notable in particular that Garbarino, in his assertion that there was an epidemic of youth violence, did not describe this as an epidemic of reported violent crime. Rather, he and others were concerned about how many boys and young men were setting off on that journey down the river, putting themselves at risk for going all the way, and losing themselves in the process. Perhaps prophetically, he was warning us that something really bad was going to happen in mainstreet America—and it did. The same year *Lost Boys* was published, two suburban high school students in Columbine, CO, attacked their school with automatic weapons and explosive devices, killing 12 of their classmates and one teacher before killing themselves. That was perhaps a watershed event for America. The urgent question became: What drove these boys/young men—with all the benefits of being White, male, and socioeconomically well off—to become murderous and apparently sociopathic so quickly?

The answer to that question was and is—"much." Risk factor profiles now exist for young men and even boys, as well as adult males both foreign and domestic. Frankly, many of these risks were already known about at the time of the Columbine massacre, but because murderous and violent youth were associated mainly with inner city gang culture, the factors that spawned sociopathic drive-by shooter behavior in young men of color received little mainstream attention.

After the Columbine shootings, the US Secret Service and the US Department of Education developed a list of violence risk factors that had seemed to contribute to that event and other school shootings. These were: 1) premeditated intent to commit violence, 2) acute stress or triggering event(s), 3) compromised mental status, 4) poor coping ability, 5) dysfunctional family dynamics, 6) limited or no school or community involvement, 7) negative or no peer group involvement, 8) abnormal interests, and 9) access to deadly weapons.[15]

Fifteen years later, all three of us continue to work with boys and young men in a variety of settings—schools, mental health clinics, residential treatment facilities, prisons. And it continues to be our assertion that there are males out there in our society that will be put at risk if continually exposed to the pervasive toxic stew of increasingly sadistic and desensitizing media-based violence and the mixed societal messages about violence (more on all of this below). They will float closer to that tipping point where *contemplating* violence becomes *acting* violently. We know through media studies that children's exposure to violent media (including television, movies, and videogames) has exponentially increased.[16] Meta-analyses of studies suggest that youth of all ages are placed at increased risk for development of adult aggressive and violent behavior when they view a high and steady diet of violent TV shows beginning in early childhood.[17]

Combine this exposure with a lack of appropriate adult guidance, particularly in the form of prosocial rites of passage, and young men move even closer to that mouth of the river. Studies in this area suggest that when youth (males and females) lack a culturally defined and universally recognized transition from adolescence into adulthood, they are placed at higher risk for violence, substance use, bullying, and delinquency. In the absence of this formalized experience, youth will attempt to create their own rites of passage through such things as dangerous risk-taking behavior and gang affiliation.[18]

Based on what we know about young men like the Columbine shooters Eric Harris and Dylan Kleebold, the Oklahoma City bomber Timothy McVeigh, the Beltway sniper Lee Boyd Malvo (aided by his older accomplice John Allen Muhammad), and more recently the Aurora theatre shooter James Holmes, the Newtown shooter Adam Lanza, and the Boston Marathon bombers the Tsarnaev brothers, these were individuals who had descended into a way-of-being that was nearly or completely disconnected from the community of fellow human beings around them, despite what their individual motives were. When that Secret Service list of violence risk factors is grafted onto these lives as they apparently were just prior to their outbursts of mass murderous violence, we see in almost all of the cases the sum total of the violence risk factors list represented. To borrow from counterterrorism jargon, they had "self-radicalized," some of them continuing to lead fairly normal surface-level lives when viewed from the outside.

So, despite the fact that a violent crime wave spurred on by youthful perpetrators did not occur as was feared, can we say that everything turned out all right despite these sporadic episodes of mass murder? Should we continue to be concerned about our young men and boys?

In a sense, it has now become a matter of exposure, desensitization, and risk—not numbers. And risk is not so much assessed by statistics as it is by survey. Current and repeated polling of young people since the 1990s reveals they view lethal or potentially lethal violence as a legitimate means by which to resolve a variety of interpersonal problems.[19] While this may simply be a representation of attitude, divorced from actual or future violent behavior, the type of random and heinous violence that we now see in America—inner-city gang warfare, suburban school shootings, and mass killings in public spaces—points to an underlying shift in our young males' views of violence. It can be argued that a line has been crossed, that old rules about when, where, and how to commit violence no longer apply. Young men without empathy, community, and humanity contemplate—and some commit—horrific acts in which all of us are potential targets—men, women, and children—in places that were previously sanctuaries like schools, faith sites, shopping malls, and public celebrations.

It is this shift in a more cold-blooded direction that the three of us are most concerned with. This may be the true epidemic—more subtle than crime statistics can detect, but nevertheless there in the qualitative experience we all have as mental healthcare providers who work extensively with boys and young men. We have a sense that we are often dealing with truly lost boys, adrift on that river— and that their numbers have grown. With more young men out there at risk, there is also more potential for that tipping point to be reached. We now have to ponder a nagging question, perhaps more often than we used to, after, say, a session with an angry, potentially violent youngster: "Is that kid going to shoot up his school/neighborhood/home?" It's a question that does not promote restful sleep at night for any of us, even though the odds are good that nothing bad will happen. It's the precedent we tend to worry about—the line that has already been crossed by others.

In the wake of the Aurora movie theatre shootings, columnist Erika Christakis blogged about "The overwhelming maleness of mass homicide."[20] In her piece, she suggested that: "Our refusal to talk about violence as a public-health problem with known (or knowable) risk factors keeps us from helping the young men who are at most risk and, of course, their potential victims." She went on to say that mass homicides may not be random and that intervention with vulnerable young men would be important, starting with an acknowledgment that this is a male problem. Subsequent comments posted by many readers accused her of criminalizing maleness and/or diagnosing maleness as mental illness.

Then in the wake of the sickening horror in Newtown, sociologist Michael Kimmel addressed the "overwhelming maleness" of the issue in his piece "Masculinity, mental illness and guns: A lethal equation?"[21] In this offering, he asserts: "Motivations are hard to pin down, but gender is the single most obvious and intractable variable when it comes to violence in America. Men and boys are responsible for 95% of all violent crimes in this country." He suggested that, for boys and young men, their definition of masculinity, as well as social learning and reinforcement around the use of violence, including retribution and "the right to annihilate" anyone who challenges their manhood, must be examined. Kimmel also received similar negative comments about stereotyping males as murderers.

The three of us do understand why some would label these perspectives as such. It *is* true that the vast majority of males in this country are not violent—certainly not homicidal—and should not be treated as if they are. But we as a society cannot ignore the fact that the vast majority of violent crime is committed by men—particularly young men. As psychologists and scientists, we cannot ignore an independent variable of such power. It would be akin to a physicist ignoring the effects of gravity in trying to explain how heavenly bodies operate in the universe.

We believe that Christakis and Kimmel are right—there is something in the way males are raised, socialized, and reinforced that puts *some* at risk for perpetrating violence or at least acting in an antisocial manner. Genetics, testosterone, and evolution do play a role, but it is the contention of many in the field of the psychological study of men and masculinity that it is mainly a socially influenced *way-of-being* driven by many factors that, depending on their effect, can either promote this type of negative behavior or protect young men from it. Suffice it to say that within our American society our boys and men are subject to a host of psychological, cultural, patriarchic, familial, media-related, evolutionary, and biological factors that influence their socialization, upbringing, and behavior. These factors will be further defined in Chapter 3.

But returning for a moment to the question posed earlier about our young men: Is it more common now at the beginning of our new century for males to come into contact with violence earlier, more often, and with more lethality? Reported violent crime statistics would suggest that it is not, but if we define "contact" as exposure in any form (through either actual or virtual experience), then the opposite may indeed be happening. Exposure and resultant attitudes in our young males are certainly not headed in a safe direction. And despite the well-known psychological principle of risk—that the best predictor of future violent behavior is past violent behavior—the trend is worrying to us. Will that principle hold up in new cohorts of young men with this heightened exposure?

BROADENING THE DEFINITION

So far, we have examined this question from a strictly street-violence and criminal perspective. However, we believe there is another significant perspective from which to consider it related mainly to legitimized/institutional violence. This would be defined for our purposes as violence that is sanctioned, regulated, rule-governed, and seen to be appropriate or even just—most clearly evidenced by war in the international arena and the death penalty domestically. Is there an

American legacy of this type of violence that may now be more pervasive and indeed growing?

Let's look at the influence of our history and our governmental/foreign policies to help answer that question. This seems most appropriate as we are just now emerging from a decade of extended twenty-first century war-fighting across two major fronts (Afghanistan and Iraq) and many minor ones.

Prior to these most recent conflicts, internationally the twentieth century was one of the most violent and destructive in all previously recorded human history, including by its mid-point two worldwide wars.[22] Not all of this was directly experienced by America, nor caused by our foreign policy, but we participated in all the major conflicts. This participation as "just war" fighters may have led to the misuse and overuse phenomenon mentioned at the beginning of this chapter. Although there are rules of war as established by the latest Geneva Convention (1949), the concept of Total War in which all aspects of an enemy's society are fair game, the development of Weapons of Mass Destruction, the rise of the military-industrial complex, and the continued use of limited war as an instrument of foreign policy could arguably be evidence of this. Our military clearly has the unparalleled ability to execute a war with impressive precision and efficiency, likely making America the envy of other competing nation-states. This may also be a source of national pride, given that, with the exception of the immediate post-Vietnam War years, the military and its veterans are generally admired.[23]

This international history and America's involvement in it seem to mirror the theme of increased individual exposure to societal violence we described above as it relates to our males. American boys and men have to some extent inherited this national history of "might makes right" and "more is better" when it comes to the application of force in the service of national interests. It may very well influence choices we make about our own behavior and reactions to things that don't sit well with us interpersonally. We (America) seem to have a history of using brute force (defensively or otherwise) to resolve international situations in our favor, despite most recently being the sole remaining superpower on the planet and arguably the biggest winner in the last worldwide conflict. Has this become a *way-of-being* for the nation that predisposes our individual males to do the same in their own lives?

Despite the fact that the twentieth century was extremely destructive and violent when compared to past centuries, some who analyze the statistics of war and conflict have reported that the peak of twentieth century violence came at its midpoint.[24] Conflict and its destructive toll have actually been declining since, which is certainly good news. However, as with reported violent crime statistics, it is once again the exposure and desensitization to legitimized violence that concern us, as well as the many lines that have been crossed in the twentieth century when it comes to the old rules of warfare. There continue to be mixed messages in our society about the use of force—and even most recently the use of coercive force through the controversial treatment of War on Terror detainees.

The exposure and desensitization are there for our boys and young men, particularly given the constant bombardment of messages they receive about war, retribution, and violent conflict resolution in the media through all electronic means, but most directly through military first-person shooter videogames (e.g., *Call of Duty, Modern Warfare,* and *Medal of Honor*). This medium, along with movies and television, seems to be promoting the elite warrior as a minimal standard for male toughness. In other words, it's not good enough to *just* join the army now—you need to become a SEAL, or a Green Beret, or an Airborne Ranger, etc. Military recruiting and advertising campaigns seek to capitalize on this interest and exposure through promotion of hypermasculine toughness combined with the use of high-tech weaponry.[25] Military psychologist

Dave Grossman has written extensively on the subject of desensitization to killing through simulators, including commercial videogames, and has concluded that this is at least partially responsible for the apparent lack of hesitation and impressive accuracy in marksmanship demonstrated by young men with no lethal violence histories who engage in mass shootings.[26]

However, what seems to be lost in this promotion of war is the testimony of men who have actually endured combat—who have taken lives with their own hands, seen people incinerated, been covered in the blood and body parts of their comrades or enemies, and who almost always lose a part of themselves physically or emotionally by the experience. To a man, they will likely tell you that this is not something that should be promoted or glorified.

We do need to acknowledge that there seems to be an internal—almost evolutionary—drive in men to seek the war experience, look forward to it, and glorify it.[27] Perhaps it is our competitive streak, our risk-taking nature, or our desire to accept a challenge. Evolutionary influences that drive violence in men can be both macro-level and genetic. One of Darwin's central assertions applies here:

> As more individuals are produced than can possibly survive, there must in every case be a struggle for existence, either one individual with another of the same species, or with individuals of different species, or with the physical conditions of life.[28]

Using violence (distinctly different than aggression—see that discussion below) to survive in the face of danger has been and will continue to be essential to our existence. That is very much ingrained in our DNA because we are the modern product of eons of human experience in this matter.

The macro-level influence comes when individual men or a society of individual men perceive that they are in endless competition with others in a world of scarce resources and hence are always wary of the threat of poaching or invasion. This tends to foster narrow aggression-based definitions of masculinity that readily shift them into perpetrating violence to protect those perceived scarce resources.[29] What would this suggest about our modern American military-industrial complex and national security apparatus? Is it national security or national "insecurity" that we are focused on?

In a world where advanced societies coexist with relatively primitive ones, are we in America (presumably advanced) playing down to nation-states like Iran or North Korea (led by men who are driven by base motivations and the raw exercise of power over people), when we engage in tit-for-tat threats and saber rattling with them? Can we rise above this unproductive, negative interaction and be secure in the fact that there are enough resources to go around (a natural fact about the world particularly if we continue to become better stewards)? An Iranian or North Korean invasion of America is highly unlikely. Their own international behavior seems driven in part by the scarcity of resources/threat of invasion focus. Why give them more fuel for that fire?

AGGRESSION VERSUS VIOLENCE

Above it was stated there is a distinction between violence and aggression. What we are proposing in this book is not an elimination of aggression—or aggressiveness. Without an aggressive response to the world around us—which in all sorts of natural ways conspires to kill us with everything from viruses to man-eating carnivores to hurricanes and earthquakes—we would very likely be extinct. Aggressiveness in the face of natural and man-made adversity keeps that from happening.

Aggression is not always synonymous with violence. For example, we are not going to blow up a virus, and we are not going to shoot or stab an earthquake. We may, however, on rare occasions need to use violence to defend ourselves or our loved ones from a bear, or a psychopath (often another man), or a maniacal dictator (again, often another man) if all else fails. This is why we have guns, park rangers, the police, and the military. We need good protectors who are ready to use violence to defend the innocent. Assertive aggression is essential to our survival (including the measured use of violence if necessary), but embracing negative violence as a *way-of-being* is not.

OTHER LEGITIMIZED FORMS OF VIOLENCE

When we view institutional violence as part of the exposure and desensitization phenomenon in our young males, we must also consider the death penalty, police brutality, and sanctioned prison violence. These are all controversial topics that are difficult to track statistically because they are subject to some additional and unique confounds that make trend analysis tentative at best. For example, the influence of the death penalty as a deterrent to violent crime may never be truly established due to the lengthy delay between the behavior (homicide) and the application of a consequence (execution), which ignores a major tenet of behavior modification with regard to the timely delivery of consequences. Also, the small national sample size of convicts who are on death row or who have actually been executed makes the statistical power of the analysis weak.[30] Other confounds exist related to police brutality[31] and prison violence,[32] including significant underreporting of incidents, lack of standardized definitions, and no means by which data is efficiently collected nationally.

Suffice it to say, however, that these things exist in our American society and are often part of the national background related to crime and punishment, authorized ways to deliver justice and keep the peace, and the treatment of inmates. Statistics that *are* available in the source material related to capital punishment, police brutality, and sanctioned prison violence suggest they all disproportionately affect racial minorities, citizens of lower socioeconomic status, the young, and/or the weak, even when controlling for all other variables.

These institutional conditions further reinforce our societal ambiguity about violence. For many of our citizens, the message seems to be: *killing and assault are illegal . . . except in cases where they are used by the government or at least condoned/overlooked by it.*

Societal ambiguity about violence also extends into the spectator sports arena, traditionally dominated by football and boxing at all competitive levels, but also professional wrestling and more recently ultimate fighting/mixed martial arts. Virtually all of these contact sports and entertainment-sports hybrids have experienced significantly increased market share in the media and in profits generated by the sale of consumer goods in recent years,[33] which would suggest that the exposure to and promotion of hypermasculinity among our young males are also greater.

Unlike the above institutionalized forms of lethal violence, these are endeavors that do not—except in rare instances—lead to lethality. However, they do involve competition through regulated violence and the physical dominance of others—activities that on the street or in other places could be considered illegal. Other themes that have been associated with these sports and their hybrids—to varying degrees—include homophobia, humiliation of opponents, and revenge/retribution.[34] These are perhaps most clearly seen in professional wrestling, which tends to overly dramatize these themes.[35]

There are arguably other examples of institutionalized or sanctioned violence in our culture that help maintain a higher level of exposure and desensitization in our young men. The above is certainly not meant to be a comprehensive list. Indeed, there are likely things on our cultural horizon that we are not even able to imagine yet, but within a few years will be hotly debated as part of the exposure and desensitization phenomenon. Such is the nature of our creative and economic freedom, and the technological engine that quickly converts ideas into things.

There is also a level of influence in our culture that potentially *promotes* violence—or at least antisocial behavior—without itself *being* inherently violent. This is evidenced through hypermasculine and misogynistic messages in music and pornography. It can also be seen in the way we in America have traditionally exploited our natural resources, pushing west in accordance with Manifest Destiny, consuming things, pushing native peoples out, and developing the land without much regard to the longer-term consequences of our actions. All of these things are important to consider as influences that we believe promote a state of arrested development in our males. These will be discussed at length in the next chapter.

SUMMARY

At the beginning of this chapter, we asked some questions that we believe are "right" to consider at this juncture in American history:

- Are violence and antisocial behavior really such big problems?
- Is it more common now at the beginning of our new century for males to come into contact with violence earlier, more often, and with more lethality?
- Have the violent youth of the late 1990s become violent adults?
- Is there still an "epidemic" level of youth violence in a new cohort?

Our discussion has ranged from the quantitative (violent crime and international conflict statistics) to the qualitative (exposure, desensitization, and subtle influence). What we can conclude is that, despite apparent decreases in reported violent crime and the death/destruction due to war, the pervasiveness of violence and violent themes in America has increased. If one accepts that exposure to violence increases the potential to become violent, then our young males continue to be at risk. There is also the troubling phenomenon of mass killing that has surfaced since the late 1990s in America, involving both domestic and international perpetrators young and old—but all males.

If we don't adequately understand why males become violent and/or antisocial in America, then our solutions may be ineffective or at best temporary in positive effect.

So what do we do about it?

With my colleagues, Drs. Ramel Smith and Héctor Torres, we have begun in earnest to campaign for a cross-cultural, male-focused examination of violence. We believe that violence in our society is a significant byproduct of the way in which boys and young men are raised/socialized, and the way in which adult men are maintained/rewarded for it. In our view, this is upstream of actual violence and hence worthy of addressing. We have given talks on the subject to audiences that nod their collective heads knowingly, perhaps a recognition that we are on to something here. They also challenge some of our views on the subject, which serves to keep us always inquiring and reflective. The fact that we are all very different looking men from different backgrounds, but saying the same things about being men in America, makes people take notice.

The three of us have not been particularly violent in our lives, but the fact is . . . we could easily *have been* if not for some intervening people and experiences. Likewise, none of us are now adherent to a stereotypical view of masculinity that keeps us stoic, materialistic, and disengaged . . . but we were all there at one point in our lives and could easily still be . . . if not for those people and experiences.

In the next few chapters, we will characterize the developmental status of men through the Masculinity Developmental Hierarchy, providing a framework upon which the Building a Better Man intervention is based.

It's Amazing What a Society Can Get Used To

Imagine you were transported back to 1955 America. It was a time of very low violence rates, very little media connectivity to promote violence, very little national enthusiasm for military adventurism, and we did not yet have enough ICBMs to wipe ourselves out. There was also a lot of inequality and a lot of protected privilege. But, relatively speaking, violence was not a big concern.

Now, imagine you woke up one morning in 1955, picked up the newspaper off your front porch, and read headlines like these:

> Violent Crime Rate up 300%
> US Imprisons 25% of World's Incarcerated Population
> 1 out of 3 Women in US Assaulted by Partners
> 1 out of 4 Women in US Raped
> Unlimited Graphic Violence and Porn Available to All Children
> Active Shooter Drills Required for All Elementary Schools

Upon seeing these, you would likely be alarmed, scared, outraged, and motivated to take action. You would contact your governmental officials immediately to demand inquiries. Committees and advisory panels would be formed at all levels of government, crisis plans would be adapted and implemented, millions of dollars would be diverted to address these absolutely unacceptable developments. It would be a classic example of the frog effect—drop a frog in a pan of boiling water and it will feel the pain instantly and immediately hop out.

But put a frog in a pan of tepid water that is slowly brought to a boil and it will stay there until it succumbs. Is this what we have come to in America? Are we all slowly boiling in the stew of violence that our men, young men, and boys have created over the years? Do we have the will to do something about it?

The "headlines" above are real and reflect the state of affairs in our country in recent years, particularly compared to the 1950s. It is incumbent on all of us to recognize that this is a significant problem and that we must address it in a systemic way. People of conscience need to coalesce around a national conversation about violence prevention, including the way in which we socialize our males.

By doing this, we may be able to coerce the frog to jump out of the pan before the water boils.

NOTES

1. World Health Organization (1996). *Violence: A public health priority*. Geneva: WHO Global Consultation on Violence and Health.
2. Garbarino, J. (1999). *Lost boys: Why our sons turn violent and how we can save them*. New York: The Free Press.

3. Federal Bureau of Investigation Uniform Crime Reports (2011). *Crime in the United States 2011*. Retrieved from: http://www.fbi.gov/about-us/cjis/ucr/crime-in-the-u.s/2011/crime-in-the-u.s.-2011.

   Department of Justice, Bureau of Justice Statistics, National Crime Victimization Survey (2011). *Criminal victimization 2011*. Retrieved from: http://www.bjs.gov/content/pub/pdf/cv11.pdf.

   Department of Justice Office of Juvenile Justice and Delinquency Prevention (2012). *Statistical briefing book*. Retrieved from: http://www.ojjdp.gov/ojstatbb/crime/jar.asp.

   Centers for Disease Control and Prevention, Division on Violence Prevention (2011). *Fatal injury reports, national and regional, 1999–2010*. Retrieved from: http://www.cdc.gov/violenceprevention/nvdrs/index.html.

4. Levitt, S. (2004). Understanding why crime fell in the 1990s: Four factors that explain the decline and six that do not. *Journal of Economic Perspectives, 18(1)*, 163–190.

5. Walmsley, R. (2011). World Prison Population List. International Centre for Prison Studies. Retrieved from: http://www.prisonstudies.org/images/news_events/wppl9.pdf.

   Abramsky, S. (2002). *Hard time blues: How politics built a prison nation*. New York: Thomas Dunne Books.

6. Federal Bureau of Investigation Uniform Crime Reports (2011).

7. Ibid.

8. Department of Justice, Bureau of Justice Statistics, National Crime Victimization Survey (2011).

9. Garbarino, J. (2001). An ecological perspective on the effects of violence on children. *Journal of Community Psychology, 29(3)*, 361–378.

   Eitle, D. & Turner R.J. (2002). Exposure to community violence and young adult crime: The effects of witnessing violence, traumatic victimization, and other stressful life events. *Journal of Research in Crime & Delinquency, 39(2)*, 214–237.

   Krug, E.G., Mercy, J.A., Dahlberg, L.L., & Zwi, A.B. (2002). The world report on violence and health. *The Lancet, 360(9339)*, 1083–1088.

10. Centers for Disease Control and Prevention, Division on Violence Prevention (2011).

11. Ibid.

12. Federal Bureau of Investigation Uniform Crime Reports (2010). *Crime in the United States 2010*. Retrieved from: http://www.fbi.gov/about-us/cjis/ucr/crime-in-the-u.s/2010/crime-in-the-u.s.-2010.

13. Brooks, G.R. & Silverstein, L.B. (1995). Understanding the dark side of masculinity: An interactive systems model. In R.F. Levant & W.S. Pollack (Eds.), *A new psychology of men* (pp. 280–333). New York: Basic Books.

14. Garbarino, J. (1999).

   Pollack, W. (1999). *Real boys: Rescuing our sons from the myths of boyhood*. New York: Owl Books.

   Kindlon, D. & Thompson, M. (1999). *Raising Cain: Protecting the emotional life of boys*. New York: Ballantine Books.

15. United States Secret Service and the United States Department of Education (2002). *The final report and findings of the safe school initiative: Implications for the prevention of school attacks in the United States*.

16. Bushman, B.J., Jamieson, P.E., Weitz, I., & Romer, D. (2013). Gun violence trends in movies. *Pediatrics, 132(6)*, 1014–1018.

17. Huesmann, L., Moise-Titus, J., Podolski, C., & Eron, L. (2003). Longitudinal relations between children's exposure to TV violence and their aggressive and violent behavior in young adulthood: 1977–1992. *Developmental Psychology, 39(2)*, 201–221.

18. Scheer, S.D., Gavazzi, S.M., & Blumenkrantz, D.G. (2007). Rites of passage during adolescence. *Forum for Family and Consumer Issues, 12(2)*. Retrieved from: http://ncsu.edu/ffci/publications/2007/v12-n2-2007-summer-fall/scheer.php.

19. Slovak, K., Carlson, K., & Helm, L. (2007). The influence of family violence on youth attitudes. *Child and Adolescent Social Work Journal, 24(1)*, 77–99.
Vernberg, E., Jacobs, A., & Hershberger, S. (1999). Peer victimization and attitudes about violence during early adolescence. *Journal of Clinical Child Psychology, 28(3)*, 386–395.

20. Christakis, E. (2012). The overwhelming maleness of mass homicide (Blog Post). Retrieved from: http://ideas.time.com/2012/07/24/the-overwhelming-maleness-of-mass-homicide/#ixzz2CQ2zRDGo.

21. Kimmel, M. (2013). Masculinity, mental illness, and guns: A lethal equation? Retrieved from: http://www.cnn.com/2012/12/19/living/men-guns-violence/index.html.

22. Ferguson, N. (2006). *The war of the world: Twentieth-century conflict and the descent of the west*. New York: Penguin Press.

23. Leal, D.L. (2005). American public opinion toward the military: Differences by race, gender, and class? *Armed Forces & Society, 32(1)*, 123–138.

24. Pinker, S. (2011). *The better angels of our nature: Why violence has declined*. New York: Viking.

25. Rutgers School of Law-Newark (2008). *Targeting youth: What everyone should know about military recruiting in public high schools*. A report prepared by the Constitutional Litigation Clinic, Rutgers School of Law-Newark. Retrieved from: http://law.newark.rutgers.edu/files/u/MilitaryRecruiting ReportConLitFinal.pdf.

26. Grossman, D. (2009). *On killing: The psychological cost of learning to kill in war and society*. New York: Back Bay Books.

27. Hedges, C. (2002). *War is a force that gives us meaning*. New York: Anchor Books.

28. Darwin, C. (1859). *On the origin of species by means of natural selection*. London: John Murray.

29. Gilmore, D. (1990). *Manhood in the making: Cultural concepts of masculinity*. New Haven, CT: Yale University Press.

30. National Research Council (2012). *Deterrence and the death penalty*. Committee on Deterrence and the Death Penalty, Nagin, D.S., & Pepper, J.V. (Eds.). Committee on Law and Justice, Division of Behavioral and Social Sciences and Education. Washington, DC: The National Academies Press.

31. Department of Justice, Bureau of Justice Statistics, Special Report (2006). *Citizen complaints about police use of force*. Retrieved from: http://web.archive.org/web/20070714134545/http://www.ojp.usdoj.gov/bjs/pub/pdf/ccpuf.pdf.

32. Vera Institute of Justice (2006). *Confronting confinement*. Commission on Safety and Abuse in America's Prisons, Gibbons, J., & Katzenbach, N. (Co-Chairs). New York: Vera Institute of Justice.

33. WR Hambrecht & Co. (2012). *The U.S. professional sports market & franchise value report 2012*. Retrieved from: http://www.wrhambrecht.com/wp-content/uploads/2013/09/SportsMarketReport_2012.pdf.

34. Messner, M. & Sabo, D. (1994). *Sex, violence, & power in sports: Rethinking masculinity*. Freedom, CA: The Crossing Press.

35. Katz, J. (2006). *The macho paradox: Why some men hurt women and how all men can help*. Naperville, IL: Sourcebooks.

3

THE MASCULINITY DEVELOPMENTAL HIERARCHY

In Chapter 2 we established that our males continue to be at risk for violence and antisocial behavior, despite a downward trend in reported violent crime. Important factors that contribute to and sustain such risk include pervasive exposure, resultant desensitization, and the reinforcing effect of mixed messages about violence within our society. Because this exposure is so pervasive, the risk is also multidetermined, meaning there are a variety of factors that influence the thought and behavior of our men and boys in a negative direction. Any given male at any given time can be swayed by a combination of factors that act on him to either maintain or alter his conception of masculinity and his subsequent behavior. Through our review of the literature and our experience as clinicians, we have identified eight of these factors—categorized as either internal or external in origin—which we believe capture a majority of this influence. While this is not an exhaustive list, the following factors are certainly present in the common experience of most American males:

- Internal: *Evolutionary, Biological, Psychological*
- External: *Societal, Cultural, Familial, Media-Related, Patriarchal.*

An important point of emphasis here is that any of these factors can act on a male in a positive (protective) *or* negative (risk) manner. Indeed, it is likely that one factor can do both at the same time. For example, a Latino man can be negatively influenced by society's interpretation of machismo as the expression and demonstration of hypermasculine characteristics, which can lead him to an overreliance on aggression or violence. Conversely, another cultural dictate related to machismo—caballerismo—with its underlying values of respect and responsibility can also influence him to act in a caring and respectful manner. While these both may be present for any given individual, it is the degree of influence that is important. Weighting these factors and their positive or negative effects for an individual can be challenging, particularly in the context of multiple factors acting on a male at the same time. In this example, the negative influence of machismo may greatly outweigh the positive or protective influence of caballerismo, if it is the family's and the community's expectation that a Latino young man be tough and/or noncommittal in relationships.

For purposes of illustration and in keeping with the theme of violence and those factors that promote antisocial behavior, in the next section we will discuss these factors primarily as negative influences on our males. We do this because we believe they are typically skewed in that direction by the demands of our modern society.

INTERNAL INFLUENCES

These are factors that predispose males to think, emote, and behave in certain ways through their genetics, physicality, and psyches. They are not typically imposed by exposure or by exerting pressure through social constructions and definitions of masculinity; rather, they are organic, natural, and at times rather difficult to change.

Evolutionary

This perspective on men and masculinity is encompassed by Darwin's seminal work, although much is going on in evolutionary psychology circles today to further the application of his theories within that field.[1] We referenced Darwin in the previous chapter, describing how aggression can be different than violence. His classic evolutionary concepts of natural selection and the elementary struggle for existence certainly have relevance for modern men. Despite improvements in the human condition and advancements in technology, particularly in the developed world, our evolutionary history continues to endow all humans with certain abilities related to surviving the natural conditions of life, surviving assaults by other species, and defending ourselves against the same from members of our own species. For men, this is thought to be manifested by superior mental rotation and vector navigation abilities, evolving from the hunter role. We also (as do women) seem to inherently know the dangers associated with other species, particularly those that are physically superior to us (e.g., lions, tigers, and bears) or have defense mechanisms that can kill or cripple us (e.g., snakes, scorpions, and other venomous creatures). We, in most cases, feel the flight-freeze-fight response in the presence of such threats and have the physical and mental ability to act on any of those survival options. It is perhaps the latter threat that we face—from other humans—that seems to be most problematic for men in particular. Males often pose dangers to other males. This is ultimately expressed through the violence of crime and warfare between individuals or groups (i.e., nation-states). Darwin believed that historically men used warfare primarily to capture women and reproductively relevant resources such as food, tools, and territory. Could this be what still drives modern warfare today? It can certainly be argued that capturing resources is a prime motivation among warring nations. This is what drove the expansion of Imperial Japan and Nazi Germany prior to World War II, and it is at least partially responsible for the involvement of oil-consuming nations in the Middle East, economically and perhaps militarily.

As far as Darwin is concerned, the struggle for mates drives males to face dangerous natural conditions, dangerous species, and engage in dangerous rivalry with other males. In the quest for mates, competition among males takes many forms, including physical contests and the derogation of competitors, but also many varied prosocial behaviors (e.g., possessing a good sense of humor, good manners, giving gifts, showing signs of commitment). Males also tend to "discount the future," meaning they live for the here-and-now, valuing immediate goods over future goods, which also applies to their relationships. Males become particularly frustrated with females who are ambiguous or deceptive in social signals related to attraction and interest. This may be an evolutionary contributor with respect to the domestic violence phenomenon.

Evolutionary psychologist David Buss, writing in the *American Psychologist*, states: "Darwin proved prescient in highlighting female choice. Women universally prefer men with economic resources, such as ambition, industriousness, social status, self-confidence, and slightly older age . . . they also prize bravery, athletic prowess . . . and other indicators of the physical ability to protect them and their children."[2] Buss concludes by suggesting that Darwin's theories of natural and sexual selection identify internal mechanisms for both women and men, and that they are "expected to differ psychologically primarily in those domains in which they have recurrently faced different adaptive problems over deep time." For men, these seem to center on aggression, but it is also true that they have other equally evolved mechanisms within them for selflessness and collaboration.

There are at least three great limitations in this discussion of evolution: 1) the assumption that gender is a binary concept, where the only two options are male or female; 2) the fact that often in these discussions gender and sex are not differentiated and these terms are used interchangeably; and 3) a heterosexist view that frequently leads to the invisibility of alternative sexual orientations and attractions when compared to the "heterosexual norm."

Regardless of the limitations of the literature, we cannot ignore that evolution has great impact on humans. Our evolutionary history has shaped us in ways that have allowed us to survive. However, the question is to what extent does it continue to influence us—particularly males with respect to aggression and violence—in this current era?

Biological

Early primate studies suggested testosterone in male primates was responsible for aggressive behavior and sexual promiscuity. However, the preponderance of recent research would suggest that, with regard to primate species, sexual behavior and aggression between males and females are similar when testosterone is manipulated as the independent variable; both groups demonstrate increased sex drive and aggression with increasing levels of testosterone.[3] Given the inherent difficulties in generalizing any primate behavior to humans, it may nevertheless be likely that the effect on human males is different or more negative due to the external factors mentioned below. It is this combination of natural internal biology and the reinforcing power of external influences that may cause a male with higher levels of testosterone to act in an excessively aggressive manner or lead to sexual aggression and/or promiscuity. There seems to be a growing catalogue of anecdotal evidence from the professional sports and entertainment-sports world in which "doping" athletes suffer behavioral side effects including aggression and violence. A notable case from professional wrestling is the Chris Benoit murder-suicide in which testosterone replacement therapy was considered to be one of the contributors to that tragedy, although there were clearly other risk factors involved as well.

Physiologically, studies have shown that men and women actually respond identically in terms of heart rate and blood pressure to the cries of an infant, and both clearly have the capacity for positive parental involvement in caregiving. Again, the mitigating effect of external reinforcement and learned behavior seems to conspire to cause men to be less effective responding to those cries when compared to women and in general to be less capable in caring for infants and children.[4]

Studies exploring the biological differences between men and women tend to conclude that the differences are not as great as we commonly think. Perhaps men and women have evolved differently based on social context, leading to some biological differences in body frame, upper body strength, and weight. But even then the differences are not that significant. Nevertheless, these slight differences may be contributing to a disparity in the use of violence among men and women in that men are more physically capable of it.

Psychological

The last of the internal influences on men's functioning is perhaps the most amenable to change, through therapy, education, or life experience. This is because the male psyche is a product of both biology *and* the external world. Modern psychological theories of masculinity are many, some having been superseded or extended by others. The general shift in theoretical orientation over time has been away from a biologic or intrinsic masculine template, to a more socially derived construct, as the following models illustrate:

1. Male Gender Role Identity Model:[5] The essential concept in this model is that "males have an intrinsic psychological nature that is deformed by modern culture and its key institutions (especially families). As a result, it is a constant struggle for men to assert and maintain their masculinity."[6] This would suggest that the demands placed on men by society run counter to their own natural state, manifested mainly by dominance, aggression, and action. Essentially, the theory states that men run into difficulty in their relationships and work when modern demands on them suppress their natural wild state.

2. Social Constructionism Model:[7] This model has been fairly dominant as a theoretical framework in gender studies, Kimmel and Messner purporting that "the important fact of men's lives is not that they are biological males, but that they become men. Our sex may be male, but our identity as men is developed through a complex process of interaction with the culture in which we both learn the gender scripts appropriate to our culture, and attempt to modify those scripts to make them more palatable."[8] In short, this suggests that males are defined by society's view of them, and this one-size-fits-all definition may or may not actually be the best fit for many. Men attempting to tailor a workable definition for themselves may find varying degrees of success in this endeavor.

3. Male Gender Role Strain Model:[9] Consistent with the social constructionist view, this model also describes the internal struggle that men experience in attempting to conform to an ideal masculine image. The model helps explain a variety of problems endemic to men: falling short of a socioculturally ideal masculine expectation—as well as the achievement of it—can lead to stunted emotional expression, anger, and even violence. According to Pleck, there are three basic outcomes by which men are trapped:

    a. Gender Role *Discrepancy* occurs when a man is not able to fulfill the ideal male role expectation due to his own emotional and physical characteristics, and other limiting factors, resulting in negative emotional/behavioral consequences such as low self-esteem and anger.

    b. Gender Role *Trauma* occurs even as a man successfully fulfills the ideal. The socialization process leading to this achievement and/or the culminating experience(s) that serve(s) as a rite of passage can themselves be traumatizing to the point where negative long-term psychological damage occurs.

    c. Gender Role *Dysfunction* occurs when a man who has successfully met the ideal masculine image struggles to maintain it. This can be seen through ongoing competition with other males in fending off their challenges and maintaining dominance. It can also be seen in the adoption of negative aspects of the ideal as a way of life, such as maintaining a low level of family participation, workaholic behavior, and emotional stoicism.

4. Developmental Trauma Model:[10] Psychoanalytic in orientation, Pollack describes a state in which: "Historically salient cultural and interpersonal models of parenting have made it likely that, as boys, men suffer a traumatic abrogation of their early holding environment; that is, a premature psychic separation from both their maternal and paternal caregivers. This is a gender-linked, normative, developmental trauma or loss that may leave boys at risk later, as adult men, for specific psychological sequelae often manifest as deficits in the arenas of intimacy, empathy, and struggles with commitment in relationships."[11] Essentially, because of the sociocultural expectation that boys must separate from their mothers, and the fact that fathers do not fill that emotional vacuum, boys become traumatized by this separation and ultimately become men with limited emotional responses (mainly anger) who feel shame about needing connection.

5. The Relational Model:[12] Also psychoanalytic in orientation, Bergman suggests that:

> A boy is placed in a terrible bind: on the one hand, he feels the pressure to disconnect for self-achievement (to be especially good at *doing* things or *fixing* things, to be competent in the world); on the other hand, he still has a strong yearning for connection. This relational paradox at the heart of normal male development (young boys becoming agents of disconnection to preserve themselves) is different from the "relational paradox" in normal female development (adolescent girls disconnecting from their authenticity to try to maintain relationship).[13]

> Essentially, when men sacrifice the relational-aspect of their being to achieve success, they create a whole host of problems typically characterized by emotional stoicism and the potential for violence and abuse at both an individual and a group/societal level. Bergman is encouraged by gender-specific efforts to reconnect men with each other (referring to the "Promise Keepers" and "Iron John" movements), but he is also concerned about men in exclusive groupings, stating that: "Of the various different groupings of human beings, men alone in groups have proven historically the most dangerous."[14]

6. The Shame-Disintegration Model:[15] Another psychoanalytic theory, Krugman suggests that:

> Normative male socialization relies heavily on the aversive power of shame to shape acceptable male behavior and attitudes and leaves many boys extremely shame-sensitive. It tends not to foster the maturation and integration of shame responses. Alongside the many ways in which boys and men respond adaptively and creatively to the evolving demands of contemporary life are male tendencies toward social and emotional isolation, patterns of compulsive work and substance abuse, and an alarming growth in the use of aggression to handle social and emotional conflict.[16]

> Boys are not taught how to integrate shame and, as men, will eventually react to it with avoidance, denial, posturing, anger, and even violence. The ultimate

insult in this regard is to be accused of un-manly behavior or to not live up to sociocultural male expectations. These reactions are either mitigated or exacerbated by significant adults (most importantly father figures) in a boy's life. They can actually be avoided and shame successfully integrated by a healthy family environment including an appropriate male role model.

Much still needs to be explored and debated with regard to psychological influences on masculinity. It is hard to separate the psyche from its environment. However, it is also important to understand how men define themselves and their masculinity, and how these definitions are influenced by their experiences and the way they internalize them.

EXTERNAL INFLUENCES

These are factors that push males to think, emote, and behave in certain ways through social learning and extrinsic reinforcement. They are typically imposed by exerting pressure via social constructions and definitions of masculinity at a number of levels. They do not originate within males, and hence their reinforcing power can *potentially* be mitigated or eliminated.

Societal

For American men and boys, the influence of *being* American cannot be overestimated. This way-of-being, so apparently distinct, popularized, and even mythologized—emulated by other men and boys around the world—may have the greatest hold on our males because of this powerful extrinsic reinforcement. That is, when a young man perceives that everyone wants to be like him, he can't help thinking that his way is the right way and possibly the *only* way to be. The notions of masculinity linked to stoicism, toughness, materialism, and dogged self-reliance are seemingly maxims of American manhood. This is certainly what is portrayed about American men in the media, and it is rooted in our history and attitude—fiercely independent, pushing out wilderness and indigenous peoples through the notion of Manifest Destiny, amassing wealth and power through individual or corporate aggression, defending what has been acquired through a culture of the gun, and being "restless in the midst of abundance" as the great observer of American society Alexis de Tocqueville asserted.[17] This "dominate-or-be-dominated" orientation—present in business, government, sports, and the military—seems to be greatly admired in our society, and those that attain dominant success in their field are held up as role models for other men.

Cultural

The population of the United States is very diverse in terms of culture, ethnicity, socioeconomic status, and other dimensions of diversity. Men and boys are influenced by specific expectations and reinforcement according to the groups they belong to and the others they are exposed to. Although there is some overlap across cultures with regard to the definition of masculinity, depending on culture there are significant nuances in the operationalization of the concept. For example, a young man will aspire to "act Black," be "macho," or "be a man," depending on his cultural identity. In general, these cultural variations on the masculinity theme are important to identify, but they are consistent in varying degrees with much of the broader societal expectations for males related to stoicism, toughness, acquisition, and self-reliance. Toughness may be the most problematic of these in that specific cultural groups of males do not tend to comingle and can often view each other as a threat. Physical, socioeconomic, and even religious differences combined with segregationist attitudes among groups may foster a fear of the "other" and tend to overshadow actual commonalities between them.

Familial

Within the milieu of societal and cultural influences, specific codes for males exist within individual families, driven by tradition and social learning passed on to sons by fathers or father figures. In cases where there are no immediate male role models, young men look to extended family members such as grandfathers, cousins, and uncles for their cues. In the absence of *any* familial male guidance, they can then look to replacement sources such as gangs, the military, or media-created role models to help define themselves and earn their manhood. It is at this familial level that the most influence may occur, simply because it is so much a part of the daily lives of boys and young men—a sustained, constant, and heavily reinforcing social learning experience. It is in the family where a boy will be taught an interpersonal approach that is either prosocial or coercive, the latter more aligned with narrowly defined masculinity maxims.

Media-Related

Whether a young man has an immediate male role model or not, the influence of modern media in shaping his understanding of masculinity can be pervasive given the multiple media outlets now available to him (e.g., television, motion pictures, videogames, and the internet). It can also be very limiting and narrow in scope, particularly since the most popular or most common depictions of men are as tough, stoic, muscular warriors who seek to avenge wrongdoing through violence. As noted in the previous chapter, ever-increasing exposure to violent media seems to have a desensitizing effect. Studies suggest that youth are placed at increased risk for development of aggressive and violent behavior when they view too many violent television shows beginning in early childhood.[18] Given the known behavioral phenomenon of desensitization, it is likely that ever-increasing access and exposure to other forms of media have a similar effect, although there has been some recent debate about the significance of violent videogames in that regard.[19] Equally pervasive are antisocial media messages and images that promote misogyny through now easily accessible pornography and some genres of music.

Patriarchal

Membership in any dominant group provides an opportunity to think myopically, act exclusively, and abuse power, particularly if that group's membership is defined by aggression, competition, and acquisition. Historically, in American and European societies, the dominant group—White men—has been reluctant to extend memberships to men of color and women. Documented abuses of power are many. Patriarchal privilege may be derived from a sense of entitlement, given that men generally assign themselves dangerous or potentially dangerous societal tasks such as soldiering, protecting, and providing. Cross-cultural studies of preindustrial societies suggest that an emphasis on warfare (i.e., aggression, competition, and acquisition) correlates positively with rigidly defined male identity and the subordination of women.[20] Societies in which there is a perceived scarcity of resources and threat of invasion also foster aggression-based definitions of masculinity.[21] To varying degrees within our patriarchal system, men are subject to this masculine code of conduct. At the same time, White male dominance in the workforce and in other institutions is decreasing as demographic changes continue to occur. More women are entering the workforce at the same time as minority groups are gaining more representative and economic power through population increases.[22] Given that it is anxiety provoking for any dominant group to relinquish power and privilege, how will White men respond to this inevitability?

As noted above, it is quite challenging to determine for any given male which of the internal and external influences are acting on him negatively or positively, and to what degree. Nevertheless, it is certainly a useful exercise to try to capture or approximate the dynamic interplay of these influences for a male if we are interested in stemming violence and increasing prosocial behavior. When we consider the problem of violence, we need to ponder this question: *Why* is there a seemingly never-ending flow of boys and young men who need this type of intervention? If we think in an "upstream" manner about this, we need to consider the weight of these multiple influences that predispose boys and young men to this behavior, from an early age. Are there broad masculinity-based explanations that seek to address this question?

MODELS OF MASCULINITY DEVELOPMENT

A review of the gender role developmental literature reveals few models specific to males in this regard, which is likely reflective of how difficult it can be to capture the multidimensional and multidetermined nature of human development over time. However, within this broad field of developmental and gender-based psychological theory, we do come across earlier work that seems to contribute specifically and most directly to a lifespan masculinity developmental model.

Bronfenbrenner's well-known ecological view of development describes the concentric multiple influences at work in human lives from childhood onward.[23] Working outward from the intimacy of the family (microsystem), to the influence of the surrounding community (mesosytem and exosystem), and then to the overarching sway of the culture (macrosystem), these pressures shape and/or maintain attitudes and behavior, particularly in the young. Bronfenbrenner also attempts to capture the effects of these systems over time (chronosystem) by describing the sociohistorical events and personal transitions across the life course of an individual. When it comes to the pervasiveness of violence and antisocial behavior in males, it seems most efficient and cost effective—from a preventative or interventional perspective—to look more closely at this ecology. At all sociocultural levels, how are we pushing our boys in the direction of violence through a narrowly defined education about what it is to be a man, and how do we then socialize them to be this way? Unfortunately, Bronfenbrenner's model is largely descriptive, so it can be limited in its value evaluating specifically how behavior is maintained or changed, and what the intrapersonal transitions are like. Nevertheless, this seminal work provides a comprehensive framework from which these descriptive systems can be further evaluated and manipulated to determine their weighting and the direction of their influence.

The Gender Role Journey developed by O'Neil et al. is another way to conceptualize the multidetermined nature of masculinity and violence, and seems to address the actual process involved more specifically.[24] It provides a conceptual framework for evaluating the inner state and behavior of an individual with regard to gender roles, sexism, and gender role conflict. Created to describe the developmental progression of both males and females, the Gender Role Journey includes five phases of personal experience across the lifespan that could result in positive change and a broadening of restrictive gender role conceptualizations. These are:

1. Acceptance of Traditional Gender Roles
2. Ambivalence
3. Anger
4. Activism
5. Celebration and Integration of Gender Roles.

The Acceptance phase implies endorsement of gender stereotypes and limited awareness of the negative aspect of this endorsement. The Ambivalence and Anger phases describe a person's progression from contemplation of change due to increased awareness, to a decision to initiate change. The Activism and Celebration phases describe the action a person takes and the intrapersonal acceptance of a new view that ultimately occurs. It is at this point that a person has accumulated enough transformative experiences of life to firmly establish a new way of thinking about gender roles and consequently a new way-of-being.

A limitation of this model is that it does not address the influences that either promote or arrest development over time, and nor is it specific to males. However, preliminary extension and application of the Gender Role Journey to men's studies have revealed that education about appropriate male/male and male/female relationships does positively impact attitudes and behavior among men. It has also been found that life experiences over time tend to challenge and broaden traditional masculinity definitions, possibly stimulating gender role phase transitions.[25] These initial findings would suggest how important it is for young men and boys—who are seemingly most vulnerable to any influence positive or negative—to be provided with education and transformative experiences that will shift their life trajectory in a prosocial direction, *before* reaching young adulthood.

The Male Reference Group Identity Dependence theory developed by Wade also describes the importance of external influences in the formation of male identity, positing that both actual experience with other men (e.g., family members and friends) and vicarious experience of the media combine to impact male behavior and psychological functioning.[26] This leads to either connection or disconnection with respect to other male reference groups that share a distinct set of norms, attitudes, and values. He also described three male identity dimensions that flow from this dual experience:

1. No Reference Group: no perceived similarity to or connection with any group of males, reflecting an undefined definition of masculinity and gender role.
2. Reference Group Dependent: perceived similarity to and strong connection with a specific group(s) of males while perceiving no commonalities with other groups, reflecting a rigid conformist definition of masculinity and gender role.
3. Reference Group Nondependent: an acceptance of and sense of connection with a variety of male groups, reflecting a broadened and nondependent definition of masculinity and gender role.

The theory emphasizes that shifts in attitude can occur dependent on context and situation, and that these are not mutually exclusive. Follow-on research suggests that the psychologically healthiest state is the latter (Nondependent), the other two tending to correlate with psychological distress, social anxiety, and gender role conflict.[27] The theory has value in that it describes the influence of external factors (risk and protective) and it implies that an individual male can change through experience and/or through situation. One limitation appears to be that the actual mechanisms of change are not clearly understood.

The Positive Psychology/Positive Masculinity (PPPM) model developed by Kiselica et al. further describes the importance of educational and transformative experiences for boys and men, emphasizing the positive masculinity approach.[28] This positive psychology framework draws upon the work of others in that field (particularly Martin Seligman), which is essentially focused on what is right and functional in people rather than what is not.[29] As such, they view PPPM as preventative, taking advantage of ten key masculine qualities that, if nurtured and emphasized as positives through education and reinforcement, can support the healthy emotional and behavioral development of males. These are:

1. Male relational style: creating relationships and friendships through shared activities and cooperative projects.

2. Male ways of caring: protecting the innocent, taking action, and expressing a range of emotions.

3. Generative fatherhood: learning and passing on fathering skills to sons and daughters.

4. Male self-reliance: considering the input of others, resisting coercion, and making reasoned decisions.

5. The worker-provider tradition of men: providing for others and taking pride in this, while balancing work and family responsibilities.

6. Male courage, daring, and risk-taking: distinguishing between sensible and foolish risks.

7. The group orientation of boys and men: banding together to foster a sense of identity and community.

8. Fraternal humanitarian service: developing social interest through volunteering and participating with others to serve the common good.

9. Male forms of humor: exchanging good-natured ribbing as a means by which to express affection.

10. Male heroism: using all of the above to live noble and wise lives, expending extraordinary effort when needed.

These positive aspects of the male way-of-being (there could be others) are critical to emphasize and teach to males when considering their lifespan development. As the authors state, "promoting the well-being of boys and men involves helping them to distinguish healthy forms of masculinity from unhealthy ones."[30] While not a stage model of development, the PPPM framework is very useful in describing the variables that foster change or progression through stages amidst the myriad of internal and external influences impacting men. In a sense, helping boys and men focus their energies on the strengths above may serve to bolster them against the negative polarities of those influences, which also has practical application in therapy for the treatment of depression and other conditions.[31] This emphasis on positive masculinity will be further elaborated in the Building a Better Man interventions later in this book.

In any developmental model, it is important to describe the sum total of ecological systems and influences, identify stages of development leading to a higher level, and the mechanisms by which this can actually occur. What we propose in the Masculinity Developmental Hierarchy (MDH) below is a model that integrates elements of these views specifically for men and boys. The MDH characterizes the polar nature (positive/negative) and importance of these variables across the lifespan. It also does not assume that a man who comfortably exists in the basic stage or phase is inherently dysfunctional. Indeed, as will be seen, many prosocial and nonviolent men can inhabit this basic level of masculinity conceptualization; these are men who lead perfectly normal and productive lives.

OVERVIEW OF THE MASCULINITY DEVELOPMENTAL HIERARCHY

Admittedly, capturing the multidimensional and multidetermined nature of variables that affect males over time is somewhat daunting. However, given the high stakes for our society in curbing violence and antisocial behavior, it is important to consider a framework that can broaden our understanding of the issue and help us make informed decisions about interventions. If nothing else, we can begin a conversation about these multiple influences, their polarity, and the combined dynamic that shapes our males' outlook and behavior.

In Figure 3.1, we depict the MDH as a pyramid, with the majority of males—typically younger—inhabiting the Dependent Acquisition stage, the lowest and most "popular" level in the hierarchy. However, as stated above, "lowest" does not necessarily imply "bad." Rather, this is a level where both nonviolent/prosocial and violent/antisocial men can coexist. It is unique in this, given that a man who is progressing through the higher stages is more likely to be primarily nonviolent and prosocial. It is also a place where all males start their journey as boys who are innately good, born into a world of influences both positive (protective) and negative (risk). It is this mix that greatly determines their course as they grow.

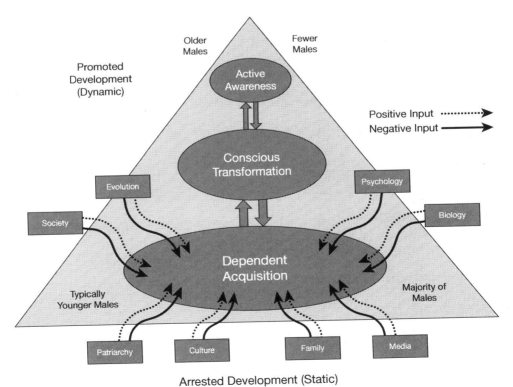

Figure 3.1 The Masculinity Developmental Hierarchy

The pyramid may be reminiscent of Maslow's well-known hierarchy of needs, describing the motivation of individuals and their developmental progression from the most basic and safety related to the more advanced or "self-actualized."[32] Like the MDH, the pyramidal shape implies that this is a progression over time that not all individuals can sustain, limiting membership of the top level to a subgroup of a population. Although Maslow is not specific about this, the pyramid also implies that there are multiple variables acting with polarity on individuals throughout each level, either facilitating or impeding motivational growth.

Similarly, movement up the MDH pyramid can be considered a motivational and lifespan process in that typically older and fewer men make that journey. However, this is not a hard and fast rule, given that men can remain in Stage One into old age, particularly if their lifestyle is functional. It may be this way as there are multiple influences (e.g., patriarchy and privilege-based reinforcement) that can maintain a comfortable status quo, arresting progress so that development is harder or does not happen at all. Violent and antisocial men may not survive into old age (due to behavioral choices that increase risk of violent premature death) or may have their freedom significantly curtailed by the legal system, if they remain in Stage One.

Table 3.1 describes the three stages within the MDH pyramid:

1. Dependent Acquisition
2. Conscious Transformation
3. Active Awareness

Table 3.1 Stages of the Masculinity Developmental Hierarchy

Stage One: Dependent Acquisition

- Acquires masculinity scripts from others and rehearses these as own
- Either unaware of or unimpressed by alternate ways of being a man
- Accepts conventional notions of masculinity, tends to endorse a restrictive view of gender roles (e.g., "be tough, be stoic, acquire things, rely on no one")
- Dependent on reinforcement of these views
- Can be either positive or negative depending on the inputs

Stage Two: Conscious Transformation

- Aware of the limitations of Stage One
- Considers a broadened view of masculinity, questions exclusivity and patriarchy
- Tolerates limited reinforcement of this questioning
- May decide to make changes

Stage Three: Active Awareness

- Accepts and maintains a broadened view of masculinity, unhindered in practicing this
- Secure with oneself despite continued limited reinforcement
- Appropriate for the common man, who may also wish to engage in activism
- Assertive, perhaps aggressive, but nonviolent

The stages are shown as distinct in both the figure and table, which may be somewhat artificial given that human change is not typically so linear. For example, a man may vacillate between stages, sometimes making significant progress but then also regressing to the previous stage depending on the dynamics of his situation and environment. His advancement may also be partial or overlap, making progress in one aspect of his life (e.g., understanding and correcting the damage caused by domestic violence) but remaining stagnant in another (e.g., succumbing to a substance addiction that can actually foster a continuation of that violence). The polarity of the variables depicted in the boxes may also shift, as would the interplay between them. This dynamic and these variables impact each of the three stages over time (which is not shown in the figure due to space limitations). Hence, a man may be able to reach the Conscious Transformation stage, but be unable to tolerate the minimized reinforcement he may receive from his fellow men, and retreat back into the Dependent Acquisition stage.

As noted earlier, the weighting of these variables and the interplay between them are difficult to accurately assess for individual men. However, it can be easier in extreme situations. For example, if all the internal and external variables are exerting a primarily positive influence on a man in Stage One, his trajectory will be vertical and accelerated. Conversely, if all those variables are exerting a primarily negative influence on him, he will likely remain in Stage One for as long as he lives. In the real world, of course, there are not many men who are solidly either of these ways. They may experience a trajectory that is accelerated at times but also prone to "navigational errors" that result in stagnation or regression. Hence, predicting their development over time is more complex.

We do know from the vast body of research in general human development that the internal variables imposed on us by nature and biology *can be* mitigated by external or environmental variables. For example, a man who is genetically predisposed to have high cholesterol can through external means reduce this to healthier levels through exercise and dietary changes. Similarly, a man who is genetically predisposed to poor self-regulation and impulsive anger can, through awareness, compensation strategies, and anger management training, mitigate this internal predisposition and avoid reactions that result in trouble and violence. The old adage once coined by Father Flanagan of Boys Town fame applies: "There are no bad boys. There is only bad environment, bad training, bad example, and bad thinking." The implication is that if the external variables acting negatively on a young man can be eliminated or shifted in a positive direction, that young man is able to become more functional. In our view, this applies to any male regardless of age and genetic predisposition.

The Dependent Acquisition Stage

This is where all men begin—as boys who learn and grow, observing their peers and the significant adults in their lives, acquiring and rehearsing what they see and what they come to believe as important in their formation as males. They are largely dependent on the reinforcement they receive from these important agents, encouraging them either to continue or to abandon certain ways of being. Ultimately, if they remain in this stage, they become men who will continue to rely on this reinforcement to one degree or another. As stated earlier, the Dependent Acquisition stage is unique in that it is most likely to contain men who are functional *and* dysfunctional, nonviolent *and* violent. Common to both is an acceptance and embracing of a rather narrowly defined, conventional notion of masculinity. These men tend to endorse a restrictive view of gender roles and for themselves may try to live the tough, stoic, materialistic, and self-reliant image of American manhood. As was described earlier in this chapter, Pleck's Gender Role Strain model suggests that this can lead to dysfunctional outcomes in that falling short of a sociocultural "macho" expectation as well as the achievement of it can potentially lead to violent and antisocial behavior, or to a lesser degree difficulty in relationships with others and limited success in advancing themselves beyond this way-of-being. Simply stated, men in this stage can be unaware of or simply unimpressed by alternate ways of being a man, and they can be quite comfortable where they are, based on the reinforcement they receive from others—male or female.

Further describing men in this stage of development could be a page-consuming endeavor, as there are many, many variations on the theme. As Pleck's model suggests, men are engaged in constant maintenance or revision of their masculine image, an image they attempt to project onto others—male and female—and the world, but with varying degrees of success. We all know men in this stage; they could be family members, friends, neighbors, or co-workers. What can often be common to all is a basic insecurity about who they are and/or dissatisfaction with their position relative to other men. This can be problematic to varying degrees. And in groups this insecurity and posturing for the benefit of others can become downright dysfunctional, as was illustrated by Bergman's quotation earlier in this chapter.

Does this mean that watching the football game with other men in your neighbor's "man cave" is going to erupt in violence or a plot to rule the world? Usually the answer is no. But, during that event an observer may witness many examples of men trying to impress other men with their words and actions. Again, the observer will likely see differing levels of success as an outcome—some men more desperate than others to establish their conventional masculinity credentials, and some men just naturally better at doing it.

There may even be others in the group who secretly yearn for a broadened interpersonal male experience, but who are hesitant to reveal this for fear of being shamed. Shame is the "S-word" that all men try to avoid experiencing religiously. As noted earlier in this chapter, Krugman's Shame-Disintegration model posits that boys are not taught how to integrate shame and, as men, will eventually react to it with avoidance, denial, posturing, anger, and possibly violence. The ultimate insult in this regard is to be accused of un-manly behavior or to not live up to sociocultural male expectations. The model also makes clear that this emotion can be used by men in an aversive manner to shape acceptable behavior and attitudes in other men. This is seen in the frequent application of shame-based motivational strategies in sports, fraternities, and in the military, where an individual's manhood is continuously challenged and questioned in an attempt to produce better performance.

Those of us who work with males in such places as residential treatment facilities or prisons are likely to see a more dysfunctional presentation of the Dependent Acquisition stage. These males are and have been subject to the same pressures noted above, but the weighting and interplay of the internal and external variables shaping their conceptualization of masculinity have contributed to their descent into violence and antisocial behavior. If they survive long enough, their behavior usually comes to the attention of the healthcare, social services, and/or legal system. Just like the more benign manifestations of the Dependent Acquisition stage described above, where men can be quite functional—working, raising families, and generally enjoying life—there are differing levels of impairment within this group. At one extreme, there are those men who are housed in endless solitary confinement in prisons, in some cases medicated with psychotropic drugs to moderate aggression, who barely see the light of day because of their dangerousness. These men are, unfortunately, unlikely to be amenable to change because of the stranglehold the negative polarity of influences has on them.

On the other hand, there are many males—young and old—in this group that are not without hope and are able to become less violent and antisocial if some key polarities are changed. It is this group that can derive the most benefit from the interventions we will describe in Part II. Again, the challenge for any of us as helping professionals is to determine for each male what those key variables are, how "upstream" they are, and how difficult it would be to reverse their polarity.

The Conscious Transformation Stage

If a man's situation and environment are such that a tipping point occurs and he is willing to consider a broadened conceptualization of masculinity, then he may begin to sample the Conscious Transformation stage. In this stage, a man becomes aware of the personal and societal limitations of being conventional and dependent on social reinforcement. He questions the exclusivity and patriarchy that maintain an unequal balance of societal power between men and women, or between men of the majority culture and the minority, and he learns about the positive aspects of masculinity that he can bring to bear on his life to either prevent dysfunction or promote change. This tipping point may be reached through an accumulation of experiences over time (e.g., living and working with minorities and women, learning in a personal way about their struggles with inequality) and/or through a limited number of transformational ones of significant impact (e.g., intensive retreats, being rescued from peril by dissimilar-looking "others"). It is through these mechanisms that fear and stereotyping fade, replaced by understanding and a realization that commonalities often outweigh differences. It is also at this point that a man must be willing to tolerate an important shift away from dependency on reinforcement from previously like-minded individuals, to less reinforcement from them. In fact, he may have to withstand criticism, misunderstanding, and possibly anger from this group. He may lose friends; he may even make enemies.

Considering this from a stages of change perspective, he would be ranging between the Contemplation, Preparation, and Action stages.[33] That is, thinking about changing and taking steps to do it would likely be dependent on the individual's tolerance for discomfort and a reordering of lifestyle. An analogy can be made to a smoker who knows he needs to stop smoking, so he finds the motivation to avoid friends who continue to smoke, changes his day-to-day habits, and finds new friends who do not smoke (or who have successfully quit). The smoking cessation literature suggests that this is the most effective way for a person to sustain abstinence from nicotine. This is likely true for a male in the Conscious Transformation intermediate stage. It would take a concerted effort to avoid people, places, and habits that would make it easy for him to slip back into comfortable old ways of being, because it is simply uncomfortable to be in limbo for very long. Human beings desire stability and resist change, so any person's tolerance for uncertainty is going to be time limited. Finding new ways of being to replace the old would be critical. To be clear, we are not implying that a conventional view of masculinity is somehow habit forming, but there would likely be a certain feeling of relief and security for a male who decided to retreat back to the man cave if he found little else to sustain him outside of it.

Hopefully, once a male has begun to look at the negative aspects of a patriarchal system, he will gain enough knowledge and support over a long enough period of time to sustain that progress and ultimately move upward. This is a particularly hard thing for most White men in American society. As discussed earlier in this chapter, it is anxiety-provoking for *any* dominant group to relinquish power and privilege. These influences produce attitudes and behaviors that loop back and tend to further reinforce men—individually and in group associations—for staying conventional.

Nevertheless, if a man is willing to consider a different way-of-being, be minimally reinforced for that, and the above arresting societal influences can be kept at bay long enough while more functional ones are developed, further vertical progression may be possible. He may be ready to embrace something more permanent.

The Active Awareness Stage

We have already established that the Conscious Transformation stage can be thought of as transitional. It is a place where a man must eventually make the choice between continuing to move up the pyramid or climbing back down into the safety of being conventional and dependent. Again, if that set of internal and external variables is acting on him in such a way that development is promoted, then he could move into the final stage—Active Awareness. As the pyramid illustration depicts, there will be fewer and typically older men at this highest level, reflecting the fact that this can be an arduous and time-consuming journey, with potentially many failed attempts before reaching the pinnacle. Nevertheless, a man who does eventually reach this stage honors the positive aspects of being a male, now accepts and maintains a broadened view of masculinity, and is unhindered in practicing it. He is secure with himself despite continued limited reinforcement and perhaps outward hostility from family members, former associates, strangers, and even the society at large. He is much less likely to resort to violence in the resolution of conflict, perhaps still valuing toughness but tempering this through wisdom and patience. He is willing to appropriately express a wider range of emotions, despite the fact that it may remain difficult for him to demonstrate this (e.g., crying without hiding it). He may become more engaged in his family, and more comfortable in assuming caretaking duties traditionally relegated to women (e.g., caring for infants, cooking meals, and cleaning the home). He also shifts his priorities from maintaining a workaholic lifestyle and being the disengaged "handyman" around the home, to maintaining healthy relationships with his partner and/or children. And perhaps most importantly, he is willing to ask for help, relying more on others and acknowledging the role of community in his life.

The Active Awareness stage is not for every American man, *but* it can certainly be appropriate for a common man. That is, one does not need to be a Gandhi or a Martin Luther King to inhabit this stage of masculinity. These famous individuals are two examples of aware men who decided to become activists, starting movements and writing their names into the history books because of their courageous stands against oppression and exclusivity within their societies at the time. This type of activism is obviously not for everyone, nor should it be. Most actively aware men can live their lives in relative anonymity; but they do things that help themselves, their relationships, their families, and their communities. A quotation from T.S. Eliot comes to mind in describing these men: "Seek the good deeds that lead to obscurity, accepting with equal face those that bring ignominy, the applause of all or the love of none." This would also imply that a man does need a certain level of courage to maintain himself in this stage, a courage that can endure a very thin reinforcement schedule, or even the possibility of attack by those men who solidly inhabit Stage One.

For ordinary men who are not a Gandhi or a King, this can mean weathering assaults on your manhood by others, including the implication that you are somehow not a man (i.e., that you are the polar opposite—a woman). But a broadened definition of masculinity replaces this view of masculinity and femininity as polar opposites. A less restrictive definition recognizes that men and women have to varying degrees attributes of both inside themselves. This would be quite difficult for a conventional male to understand or accept, as it has been ingrained in him that he is one or the other, dependent on his behavior and reputation. It is easier for a male in the highest stage to conceptualize masculinity and femininity as a continuum, with all people able to locate themselves somewhere in between extreme versions of both. Thinking about it in terms of the bell curve, most people would be solidly in the middle of the continuum, with fewer and fewer toward either pole. A man—especially a younger man—in this stage must also be willing to endure being referred to as gay. In boyhood, this is an insult of the highest degree, likely higher than disparaging remarks about one's mother. It will almost guarantee a shame-based violent reaction. Again, this relates back to the erroneous notion that we as males are "either/or" propositions—100% or 0%, based on our anatomy and the narrow sociocultural definition of what that means.

Regarding the notion of courage, it should not be assumed that an actively aware man has given up assertiveness and aggression. History reveals that even Gandhi and Martin Luther King were very much this way in their work. They knew the value of dogged assertiveness and aggressiveness in pursuing their aims. They advocated civil disobedience as an aggressive response to oppression and inequality. A common man inhabiting this stage is similar, but perhaps not as willing to resist the temptation of using violence to solve a problem. After all, most men are very good at getting angry and acting on that anger, sometimes in a violent manner. Stage Three men are not immune to this, primarily because it is such an accepted emotion in the narrow conceptualization of masculinity that most of us have had inculcated in us from an early age. The point in Stage Three is that men can be assertively aggressive, honoring those positive aspects of manhood, but they should always strive to avoid the negative aspects of aggression that can lead to violence and antisocial behavior, resisting the temptation to regress and climb back down the pyramid. Indeed, it is likely that a man who has maintained himself at this highest level would find upon his return to the Dependent Acquisition stage that he was a bit of a stranger in a strange land.

SUMMARY

We have just described a model that attempts to capture the dynamic and multidetermined nature of American masculinity and a male's ability to navigate his way through its stages of change. As stated above, it is quite challenging to determine which variables, at which times, and in which ways (positive or negative) promote or arrest development for any given male. A model gives us a starting point to consider this with perhaps a modicum of predictive power.

The question again needs to be asked: "*Why* is there a seemingly never-ending flow of males who need intervention to correct violent and antisocial behavior?" When we consider as a goal violence reduction and an increase in prosocial behavior among this group, we need to consider a gradual and sustainable shift in their ecology—the internal and external variables that are constantly acting on them in a complex interplay of polarities. At this point in American history, this ecology seems skewed toward maintaining a narrowly defined conceptualization of masculinity, which of course results in all kinds of dysfunction for our males. These were described at length in Chapter 2 and referred to in this chapter.

Even a cursory literature review reveals a plethora of programs, strategies, and interventions that can effectively reduce bullying, conflict, and violence among boys, young men, and older men. This has become a growing interventional focus in the field of psychology, sociology, and public policy in recent years. Many of these ideas are theoretically sound and empirically validated, and can be adopted by a variety of agencies, such as schools and prisons, to help males who have already become problematic in this regard.

In moving now from problem identification/description to problem resolution in Part II, we will incorporate many of these empirically validated preventative and interventional approaches into a comprehensive Building a Better Man program within the context of the MDH, as we believe this is the key to effectively addressing the violence and antisocial behavior of our males in American society.

Shifting our skewed ecology for our males should always have as its goal the promotion of vertical movement up the MDH pyramid or, secondarily/ minimally, the achievement of a stasis within Stage One that ensures a minimum level of nonviolent and prosocial behavior. The latter was most eloquently stated by an inmate who recently completed one of our workshops in his prison. He was asked how he would live his life differently once he was released. His response: "I'm not gonna do anything different for myself or my community, but I will be one less person to fear walking down the street." In many cases, this can be a real success story because the potential end result is a statistical decrease in violence.

This effort should at its core be focused on *protecting, educating, and connecting* our vulnerable boys and young men in American society. Vulnerability is not a function of low socioeconomic status. It is a condition that all boys find themselves in regardless of their station in life. As noted earlier, the pressure on men—particularly young men—to demonstrate and maintain a tough, stoic, materialistic, and self-reliant expression of manhood is tremendous. Threats to this unrealistic ideal abound in the ecology of all males and require nearly constant vigilance. Clearly, though, many young men who are minorities and living in low socioeconomic communities are more susceptible to fatal violence— either as victims or perpetrators, or both.

But being young and vulnerable can be a good thing. Behavioral science tells us that it is much easier to teach a new skill than to reverse a bad behavior. Young people are the "unformed clay" where this is easiest to accomplish. It is better to avoid the development of a bad habit than to try to reverse one. That would suggest that we focus on shepherding our young males through their developmental years so as to maximize their potential to progress up the MDH pyramid. Addressing the societal problem of violence early in the lifespan of males reduces the need for seemingly endless "downstream" interventions. Essentially, society would get more return on its investment.

The ultimate goal of an upstream or ecological approach to protecting, educating, and connecting boys and young men is to foster *sustained* violence reduction, while still honoring the positive aspects of male socialization. This could pay dividends not only on an individual level but, over time, also on a societal one in which there is less perceived need to categorize other men or groups of men as a dichotomous "friend or foe." Whether this shift will result in less racial, institutional, or even international violence over time remains to be seen, but it seems certainly worth the effort when we consider the relative ease with which individuals, groups, or even nations currently engage in violence, this in an era in which weapons (including weapons of mass destruction) are more and more prevalent.

NOTES

1. Darwin, C. (1859). *On the origin of species by means of natural selection.* London: John Murray.
2. Buss, D.M. (2009). The great struggles of life: Darwin and the emergence of evolutionary psychology. *American Psychologist, 64(2)*, 144.
3. Smuts, B., Cheney, D., Seyfarth, R., Wrangham, R., & Struhsaker, T. (Eds.) (1987). *Primate societies.* Chicago, IL: University of Chicago Press.
4. Jones, C.L., & Thomas, S.A. (1989). New fathers' blood pressure and heart rate: Relationships to interaction with their newborn infants. *Nursing Research, 38*, 237–241.
5. Pleck, J.H. (1995). The gender role strain paradigm: An update. In R. Levant & W. Pollack (Eds.), *A new psychology of men* (pp. 11–32). New York: Basic Books.
6. Ibid., 26.
7. Ibid.
8. Ibid., 21.
9. Ibid.
10. Pollack, W.S. (1995). No man is an island: Toward a new psychoanalytic psychology of men. In R. Levant & W. Pollack (Eds.), *A new psychology of men* (pp. 33–67). New York: Basic Books.
11. Ibid., 35.
12. Bergman, S.J. (1995). Men's psychological development: A relational perspective. In R. Levant and W. Pollack (Eds.), *A new psychology of men* (pp. 68–90). New York: Basic Books.
13. Ibid., 75.
14. Ibid., 86.
15. Krugman, S. (1995). Male development and the transformation of shame. In R. Levant and W. Pollack (Eds.), *A new psychology of men* (pp. 91–126). New York: Basic Books.
16. Ibid., 93.
17. Tocqueville, A. (1840). *Democracy in America.* London: Saunders & Otley.
18. Huesmann, L., Moise-Titus, J., Podolski, C., & Eron, L. (2003). Longitudinal relations between children's exposure to TV violence and their aggressive and violent behavior in young adulthood: 1977–1992. *Developmental Psychology, 39(2)*, 201–221.
19. Ferguson, C.J. (2013). Violent video games and the supreme court: Lessons for the scientific community in the wake of Brown v. Entertainment Merchants Association. *American Psychologist, 68(2)*, 57–74.
20. Ross, M.H. (1985). Internal and external conflict and violence: Cross-cultural evidence and a new analysis. *Journal of Conflict Resolution, 29*, 547–579.
21. Gilmore, D. (1990). *Manhood in the making: Cultural concepts of masculinity.* New Haven, CT: Yale University Press.
22. US Census Bureau (2011). Current Population Survey. Annual Social and Economic Supplements. Retrieved from: http://www.census.gov/hhes/www/poverty/publications/pubs-cps.html.
23. Bronfenbrenner, U. (1979). Contexts of child rearing: Problems and prospects. *American Psychologist, 34*, 844–850.
    Bronfenbrenner, U. (1986). Ecology of the family as a context for human development: Research perspectives. *Developmental Psychology, 22*, 723–742.
    Bronfenbrenner, U. (1989, April). *The developing ecology of human development.* Paper presented at the Society for Research in Child Development meeting, Kansas City, MO.

24. O'Neil, J. & Egan, J. (1992). Men's and women's gender role journeys: A metaphor for healing, transition, and transformation. In B. Wainrib (Ed.), *Gender issues across the life cycle*. New York: Springer Publishing.

    O'Neil, J., Egan, J., Owen, S., & McBride Murray, V. (1993). The gender role journey measure: Scale development and psychometric evaluation. *Sex Roles, 28(3/4)*, 167–185.

25. O'Neil, J. & Egan, J. (1992). Men's gender role transitions over the lifespan: Transformations and fears of femininity. *Journal of Mental Health Counseling, 14*, 305–324.

26. Wade, J. (1998). Male reference group identity dependence: A theory of male identity. *Counseling Psychologist, 26(3)*, 349–383.

27. Wade, J., & Brittan-Powell, C. (2000). Male reference group identity dependence: Support for construct validity. *Sex Roles, 43(5/6)*, 323–340.

28. Kiselica, M.S. & Englar-Carlson, M. (2010). Identifying, affirming, and building upon male strengths: The positive psychology/positive masculinity model of psychotherapy with boys and men. *Psychotherapy Theory, Research, Practice, Training, 47(3)*, 276–287.

29. Seligman, M. & Csikszentmihalyi, M. (2000). Positive psychology: An introduction. *American Psychologist, 55(1)*, 5–14.

30. Kiselica, M.S. & Englar-Carlson, M. (2010), 284.

31. Sweet, H. (2012). Counseling depressed men: Making darkness visible. In H. Sweet (Ed.), *Gender in the therapy hour: Voices of female clinicians working with men* (pp. 171–195). New York: Routledge.

32. Maslow, A.H. (1954). *Motivation and personality*. New York: Harper & Row.

33. Prochaska, J.O. & DiClemente, C.C. (1983). Stages and processes of self-change of smoking: Toward an integrative model of change. *Journal of Consulting and Clinical Psychology, 51(3)*, 390–395.

PART II

BUILDING FROM THE GROUND UP

CHAPTER 4

EFFECTIVE VIOLENCE PREVENTION STRATEGIES

Violence is an extremely broad concept; it vastly differs in terms of demographics (age, color, ethnicity), methods (genocide, sexual abuse, bullying), types (self-inflicted, interpersonal, collective), motivation (survival, boredom, group pressure), and context (gang related, domestic, war). This is in part why the literature on violence prevention is extensive, complex, and at times fragmented. Factors contributing to this fragmentation include differences of opinion about what constitutes legitimate documentation of violence (e.g., arrest reports versus citizen reports), gaps in data collection, and theoretical differences (e.g., behavioral versus psychodynamic conceptualizations). As a result, educators, service providers, and academics often find it difficult to reach clear conclusions about the most effective prevention measures. A summary of the existing literature on violence prevention is an ambitious task and outside the scope of this chapter. In this review, we highlight the literature that provides a foundational understanding of violence prevention and examine existing practices that have proved effective at reducing and preventing violence. Lastly, we conclude this chapter with a brief introduction to our program and highlight some of its science-based practices.

DEFINING VIOLENCE

As noted previously in Chapter 2, the World Health Organization (WHO) defines "violence" as: "The intentional use of physical force or power, threatened or actual, against oneself, another person, or against a group or community, that either results in or has a high likelihood of resulting in injury, death, psychological harm, mal development or deprivation."[1]

Violence is commonly divided into three subtypes: (1) self-directed (e.g., suicide and other forms of self-inflicted harm), (2) interpersonal or between individuals (e.g., domestic violence and assaults by strangers), and (3) collective (e.g., violent incidents committed by large groups of individuals such as war).[2] All three subtypes can be inflicted through the following four methods: (1) physical force, (2) sexual assault, (3) psychological attack, and (4) deprivation.[3] Given the focus of our program, the discussion in this chapter pertains to interpersonal violence.

Violence is a phenomenon that has plagued every society since the beginning of the human race and is the leading cause of death worldwide for people aged 15–44 years.[4] From genocide to bullying, all forms of violence inevitably lead to regrettable consequences. Death is the ultimate consequence, but violence at any level can negatively impact the quality of life, health, and economy of those around it, including the victims, perpetrators, family members, and communities.

A large portion of the literature focuses on children and youth, as childhood aggression has been linked to adult violence.[5] Prevention efforts tend to target the youth population, as the most common victims and perpetrators are young people.[6] However, it is important to note that most individuals who commit an act of violence do not engage in repeated violent behavior throughout their lives.[7]

It is very difficult to predict violent behavior, as the underlying motives vary depending on the situation and individual; however, certain situational factors do play an important role in determining whether individuals will be more prone to engage in violent behavior. Krug and colleagues listed the following as some of the most common situational factors: (1) specific motivation, (2) location of the incident, (3) presence of alcohol or weapons, (4) persons present, and (5) whether the individual is engaged in another activity that can trigger violence, such as burglary.[8] Specific motivation varies depending on the age of the individual. Younger people tend to be motivated by a need for excitement, while adults tend to be more utilitarian, meaning the violence has a specific purpose.[9]

Violence has been conceptualized as a public health problem which can be prevented by addressing the contributing factors, as in the prevention of infectious diseases.[10] Some research has found a positive correlation between violence and other behavioral problems such as risky sexual behavior and illicit substance abuse, among others.[11] Therefore, understanding the factors that make individuals more or less vulnerable to engaging in violence is an essential part of developing and implementing effective violence prevention measures.

RISKS AND PROTECTIVE FACTORS ASSOCIATED WITH VIOLENCE

Multiple sources have empirically identified variables that contribute to the increased likelihood that an individual will engage in an act of violence and may also be predictive over the long term.[12] Such variables are commonly known as risk and protective factors. Risk factors may not be the direct cause of violent behavior but are closely related. In other words, when risk factors are present, the probability that violence will occur increases. On the other hand, the presence of protective factors tends to decrease the likelihood of violence. Unfortunately, protective factors have not been studied as extensively and thoroughly as risk factors; further research about the mitigating effect of these influential elements is needed.

Understandably, most prevention initiatives target both sets of factors in an effort to decrease the likelihood of future violence. Given that violence is not solely a problem of the individual but a problem that impacts and can be sustained by multiple socioecological systems, we agree that prevention initiatives should address the accumulation of risk factors across multiple levels of social systems.[13] Consistent with Bronfenbrenner's model,[14] researchers have made an effort to understand risk and protective factors in young people from a socioecological point of view, classifying them as individual, family, peer/social, community, and social. Below is a list of those factors most commonly cited in the violence prevention literature.[15]

Individual risk factors: gender; attention deficit and/or poor concentration; hyperactivity or poor impulse control; sensation seeking and risk-taking characteristics; low IQ and/or learning disorders; deficits in social cognitive or information-processing abilities; low educational attainment; history of aggressive behavior; drug, alcohol, or tobacco use; high emotional stress; history of treatment for emotional problems; antisocial beliefs and attitudes; history of violent victimization; and exposure to family violence and conflict.

Family risk factors: minimal parental involvement or supervision; lack of emotional attachment to parents or caregivers; harsh, lax, or inconsistent disciplinary practices; physical and/or verbal abuse; low parental education and income; parental substance abuse or criminality; and family dysfunction.

Peer and social risk factors: association with delinquent peers; involvement in gangs; rejection by peers; lack of involvement in conventional activities; poor academic performance; and disinterest in schoolwork and school activities.

Community risk factors: diminished economic opportunities; high concentrations of low-income residents; high level of transiency; high levels of family disruption; low levels of community participation; the presence of gangs, guns, and drugs; and socially disorganized neighborhoods.

Social risk factors: income inequality; racism and other forms of oppression; lack of policies offering social protection or failure to enforce those policies; and exposure to violent media sources, particularly if these depict violence as an appropriate method to cope with and resolve conflict.

Individual and family protective factors: intolerant attitudes toward deviance; high IQ; high grade point average; positive social orientation; religiosity; connectedness to family or adults outside the family; ability to discuss problems with parents; high parental expectations about school performance; shared activities with parent/s; consistent presence of parent at mealtimes and after school; parental supervision; participation in social activities; and a strong racial/ethnic identity.

Peer and social protective factors: availability of role models and positive relationships; commitment to school; safe and predictable environments; and participation in positive social and prosocial activities.

These are general risk and protective factors; an in-depth examination of specific contexts and forms of violence is needed in order to also identify specific risk and protective factors associated with different types of violence before attempting to implement corrective measures. For example, in the context of domestic partner violence, it is essential to understand that economic stress and marital conflict are both common contributors.

The presence of certain risk factors and the absence of protective factors is not a mandate for violence. Rather, these variables may interact with, increase, or decrease the probability of violence. These factors aid in the development of prevention initiatives in terms of populations to target, skills to develop, and areas in need of change. Furthermore, identifying these factors can broaden our perspective and help us avoid focusing solely on the individual's "deficiencies" and lack of control. The list of socioecological factors may facilitate this process, as it tells us that some individuals who defer to violence may live in unjust and inhumane conditions over which they have little or no personal control. For example, James Diego Vigil has discussed how the multiple marginalities faced by Latino youth (racism, living in poverty, lack of supervision, and inadequate institutional assistance, among other social structural challenges) create conditions that facilitate street socialization and gang involvement.[16]

EVALUATION OF VIOLENCE PREVENTION INITIATIVES

Scientific literature can be extremely helpful in identifying prevention practices with solid empirical evidence of effectiveness and ineffectiveness. Engaging in practices lacking empirical support, even those that are well intended, can waste resources and lead to greater harm. At the same time, the literature needs to be looked at from a critical viewpoint, as on occasion it has produced inconsistent results. For example, some articles point to statistics which indicate the lack of effectiveness of domestic violence prevention initiatives,[17] while others reveal positive results in the overall decrease of domestic violence using randomized control trials of treatment groups consisting of male perpetrators.[18] Regardless of these difficulties, there is enough evidence to support the idea that violence can be prevented by implementing specific prevention practices.[19]

Numerous studies have attempted to evaluate violence prevention initiatives by measuring individuals' changes in attitudes. It is accepted that intentions are connected to actions; however, a change in attitude does not guarantee a change in violent behavior. Effective initiatives should produce long-term results, both in attitude and behavior; thus it is important to look at behavioral changes over time. For example, initiatives based solely on sharing information do not tend to have long lasting effects on violent behavior.

An additional challenge in the evaluation of violence prevention initiatives is that research often focuses on one or a few factors in isolation, and neglects to explore the dynamic interactions among the ecological factors contributing to violence. Recognizing these factors at an individual level can be an essential component, as measures that may be effective within a specific group or population may not be effective for others. In 2010, the WHO released a report entitled *Violence Prevention: The Evidence*, a meticulous review of scientific violence prevention literature.[20] The report organizes violence prevention strategies into seven categories and analyzes the evidence supporting the effectiveness of specific initiatives within each category. Below is a brief summary of each of these:

1. *Developing safe, stable, and nurturing relationships between children and their parents and caregivers.* Overall, parenting programs offered strong evidence of effectiveness in reducing child maltreatment; aggressive, disruptive, and defiant behavior in children; and arrests, convictions, and violent acts among adolescents and young adults.

2. *Developing life skills in children and adolescents.* Initiatives that focus on the development of life skills demonstrated strong efficacy in preventing violence. "Life skills" have been understood as cognitive, emotional, interpersonal, and social skills that help a child or adolescent deal effectively with everyday life challenges. Life skills training seeks to foster positive self-awareness, self-management, social awareness, relationships, and decision making. The evidence demonstrates that these initiatives are most effective when implemented early in an individual's life. In addition to helping reduce violence, life skills training can reduce other risky behaviors such as substance abuse and reckless sexual activity. Moreover, these programs can positively impact children and adolescents' prosocial behavior, educational attainment, and employment prospects. And perhaps most importantly, the report presents evidence that the impact these programs have on youth can be sustained into adulthood.

3. *Reducing the availability and harmful use of alcohol.* It is well established that alcohol contributes to violence. The report presents strong evidence that initiatives aimed at alcoholics and binge drinkers decrease domestic violence,

child maltreatment, and suicide. Other measures, such as regulating the price and sale of alcohol, have the potential to produce positive results, but the research is limited, especially in developing countries.

4. *Reducing access to guns, knives, and pesticides.* This category lacks evidence in some areas; however, the overall findings are promising. The report suggests that initiatives that attempt to reduce access to weapons, such as national legislation, can help reduce violence. Violence through the use of weapons must be tackled from a systemic perspective that incorporates poverty, social inequalities, illegal drug trades, and criminal justice systems.

5. *Promoting gender equality to prevent violence against women.* The report asserts that promoting gender equality is an essential part of violence prevention. Given that gender inequalities increase the risk of violence against women, as in the case of domestic violence, initiatives that promote gender equality and challenge stereotypes can decrease violence against women. School-based programs that address this have shown to effectively reduce dating violence and change attitudes toward violence.

6. *Changing cultural and social norms that support violence.* Social and cultural norms can support and encourage violence; however, initiatives that challenge such norms can also reduce or prevent it. These types of initiatives, including advertisements and marketing with positive social messages, have been widely used but not widely studied, mainly due to the difficulty of attributing outcomes solely to them.

7. *Victim identification, care, and support programs.* The last section of the report addresses initiatives that support and protect victims of interpersonal violence. These include advocacy, counseling, referrals, and safety planning— all of which have been shown to effectively increase victim safety and reduce the likelihood of further harm. In addition, these initiatives not only directly protect victims but can also help end the cycle of violence for future generations by having a direct impact on the children involved in these types of situations. The evidence is promising but limited, primarily due to inadequate research in developing countries and a lack of studies demonstrating positive long-term effects.

Matjasko and colleagues also attempted to abridge and generate clear-cut conclusions from the literature in a systematic meta-review of youth violence prevention programs.[21] The authors conducted 37 meta-analyses and 15 systematic reviews of behavioral and psychosocial programs in order to identify effective strategies available in the field. They classified the strategies into five categories, based on the types of programs included in the review: (1) general, (2) treatment-specific, (3) family based, (4) school based, and (5) community based.

Prevention strategies are generally classified as Universal, Selective, or Indicated. Universal prevention strategies do not incorporate risk factors, but target a population such as a school or community. Selective prevention strategies target subgroups of the general population which are "at risk" because of the group they belong to, such as children of violent parents. Indicated prevention strategies target individuals who have been identified as being "high risk," because they have either displayed early signs of aggression or have already engaged in violent behavior. The results of the meta-review indicate that Selective and Indicated prevention strategies were the most effective, which speaks specifically about the population the strategy targets. This may be due in part to the fact that initiatives employing Universal strategies do not clearly define the individual's need and applicability, whereas a Selected or Indicated strategy may facilitate an individual's understanding of how it is personally relevant.

The results of this meta-review also indicated that family initiatives, including parent training, are viable in preventing aggression and other antisocial behavior, specifically for children over the age of three. In terms of treatment-specific initiatives, the review found that cognitive-behavioral therapy (CBT) and multi-systemic therapy (MST) had moderately positive effects. The authors emphasized that when implementing complex treatments such as CBT and MST in community settings, careful attention should be given to high-quality implementation in order to ensure treatment fidelity. In terms of school-based programs, the meta-review identified behavior modification and peer mediation programs as the most effective. In community-based programs, the authors found moderate positive effects were related to the specific program type or their specific components. They explained that even though community afterschool programs involving evidence-based interventions were found to be effective, this was not the case for all afterschool programs. This underscores the importance of using strategies with data supporting their effectiveness.

Both studies provide a global perspective on violence prevention and the effectiveness of current initiatives, but are limited by the minimal amount of research that has been conducted in rural areas and underdeveloped countries, inadequate details concerning the methods employed in the reviewed research, and the lack of emphasis on issues related to identity and oppression. Given that a strong sense of identity can be a protective factor, initiatives that aim to develop or sustain a healthy identity (racial/ethnic, gender, and sexual, among others) and address the impact of oppression on certain populations should be included in such analyses. Another significant limitation of the studies on children is that they were conducted in schools. The findings may not incorporate data about children who are not in school for various reasons, which, if included, could skew the results.[22] Nevertheless, these two reports are remarkable in their scope, and the results are extremely useful in identifying effective violence prevention initiatives.

VIOLENCE PREVENTION AMONG MALES

Because males have been identified as the gender which disproportionately engages in violence, it is vital to focus on them in violence prevention efforts.[23] Their role in prevention could range from abstaining from violence to actively addressing the root of it in themselves or others.[24] However, engaging men in prevention programs and initiatives does not come without challenges.

A major challenge is overcoming their generalized tolerance for violence. Such tolerance not only facilitates its use as a coping mechanism, but can also decrease the likelihood that men will actively intervene in acts of violence by others. In addition, a consequence of such tolerance is that it facilitates a perception of violence as an acceptable way to cope, limiting the use of alternative, more effective coping skills. Finally, as previously discussed through our Masculinity Developmental Hierarchy, the social construction of hegemonic masculinity has led many men to experience difficulty in acknowledging and expressing emotions other than anger, which in turn leads them to be explosive and impulsive in their expression of anger.

In an overview of the literature on men and violence conducted by Berkowitz,[25] he discusses the following nine assumptions commonly shared by programs found to effectively prevent violence among men:

1. It is important that men assume their role in and responsibility for preventing violence.

2. It is more productive if men are engaged in solving the problem, rather than constantly being labeled as the problem.

3. Although mixed gender groups can be effective, male initiatives facilitated by men are more appropriate for two reasons: first, violence prevention goals differ between genders and, second, men are more likely to be influenced by other men.

4. The initiatives should encourage an honest and interactive discussion of feelings, ideas, and beliefs.

5. There should be a forum to critically discuss notions of masculinity, including how it relates to male privilege, sexism, heterosexism, and violent behaviors.

6. Skill development is essential, including how to intervene when other men are engaging in violence.

7. The initiatives should assist men in developing antiviolence attitudes.

8. The initiatives should assist men in learning how to be healthy and make healthy choices.

9. The initiatives should be influenced by and in harmony with the work done by women advocates, educators, and prevention specialists.

DIVERSITY AND VIOLENCE PREVENTION

The term diversity is broad and encompasses multiple factors including race, gender, sexual orientation, and physical and mental ability, among others. A great asset of the United States is its diversity; the country is, has been, and will continue to be home to individuals from diverse national, ethnic, and racial backgrounds. However, significant segments of the population, particularly individuals of color, continue to be marginalized and afforded insufficient access to basic needs such as safe housing, education, healthcare, and employment opportunities.

Racial disparities are real and well documented. The unequal treatment and marginalization of people of color have contributed to the existence of racial disparities in healthcare, education, and socioeconomic status. Healthcare disparities, for example, include lack of health coverage, difficulty accessing services, and prevalence of certain medical conditions. In 2011, while 87% of the Caucasian population under the age of 65 had health insurance, only 66% of American Indians and Alaska Natives, 69% of Latino/as, 81% of African Americans, and 84% of Asian Americans were insured.[26] As a result, many minorities do not receive the necessary health services and may be diagnosed at advanced stages of their illnesses.[27]

Other disparities are extensive and include the following:

Healthcare
*   American Indians, African Americans, and Latino/as have a higher risk of contracting diabetes than Caucasians.[28]
*   Latina women are twice as likely to contract cervical cancer than Caucasian women.[29]
*   African Americans have the highest rate of asthma and asthma-related illnesses among all racial groups.[30]
*   African Americans have higher diagnoses of and mortality rates from preventable and treatable types of cancers.[31]
*   African Americans have higher death rates from heart disease, strokes, cancer, asthma, influenza and pneumonia, diabetes, and HIV/AIDS than do Caucasians.[32]

- American Indians and Alaska Natives adults are 60% more likely to have a stroke than Caucasian adults.[33]
- Native Hawaiian infant mortality rates are higher than those of any other racial group.[34]

Education

- Students of color attend schools with fewer resources than schools attended by Caucasian students.[35]
- The highest dropout rate is among Latino/as, followed by African Americans and American Indians/Alaska Natives.[36]
- In 2010, 63% of Hispanics and 84% of African Americans had a high school diploma, in comparison to 88% of Caucasians, and 14% of Hispanics and 20% of African Americans had a bachelor's degree or higher in comparison to 30% of Caucasians.[37]

Economic

- In 2011, the average family median income for African American families was $32,229 and $38,624 for Latino families, compared to $55,412 for Caucasian families.[38]
- In 2011, 28% of African Americans, 28% of American Indians, 25% of Hispanics, and 17% of Native Hawaiians/Pacific Islanders were living at the poverty level, in comparison to 9.8% of non-Hispanic Caucasians.[39]
- In 2011, the unemployment rate for African Americans was 15.8%, compared to a 7.9% unemployment rate for Caucasians.[40]

Legal

- African Americans and Latino/as are more likely to be stopped by the police,[41] incarcerated, and receive longer sentences than Caucasian individuals.[42]
- Currently, more than 60% of the individuals in prison are people of color.[43]
- Approximately one in every ten Black males in their thirties is in a correctional institution.[44]

The Department of Health and Human Services' Office of Minority Health (OMH) asserts that one way to help eliminate these inequities is by providing culturally competent and linguistically appropriate services.[45] Cultural competence has been defined as behaviors, attitudes, and policies that lead to effective work with diverse populations.[46] An overview of the concept and how to develop cultural competence is outside the scope of this chapter; however, the importance of developing the knowledge, skills, attitudes, and experiences that lead to culturally competent services cannot be underestimated. A culturally competent service provider must continually be aware of his/her own assumptions, biases, and limitations; make considerable efforts to understand the worldview of diverse populations; develop and practice effective strategies for working with diverse populations; and advocate for the needs of those whom they work with.[47]

In order for providers to deliver effective and culturally appropriate services to minority individuals with diverse backgrounds, providers must tailor their services to acknowledge and appropriately address oppression and racial disparities. Furthermore, culture informs individuals' understanding of the world, as well as their thoughts, identity, and behavior; therefore, it is crucial that providers are aware of participants' worldview and cultural values in order to better understand their thoughts and beliefs associated with violence and violent behavior. For example, when working with Latino men, a deep understanding of the concept of "machismo" is necessary. Machismo tends to be immediately associated with negative characteristics such as aggression and sexism. Rather than focusing on the negative aspects, service providers should examine the historical notions that influence the general population's perception of this concept as against the participants' perception, which may include the value of "caballerismo," a term associated with positive affiliation, ethnic identity, problem-solving and coping skills.[48]

Violence prevention initiatives must be culturally relevant and appropriate in order to be effective, fair, and accurate.[49] Therefore, in order to address the foundations of aggression and violence and introduce preventative initiatives, a thorough knowledge of the current systems of oppression and resulting disparities is necessary. For example, arrest rates can be interpreted as African American men engaging in violent crimes more frequently than any other racial group, which reinforces stereotypes about this population. However, data indicate that African American men are not more violent than the general population, and that race does not increase the tendency for violent behavior, which implies the justice system disproportionally targets and profiles the African American population.[50] In our prevention work we cannot ignore that African Americans face greater stigma attached to their expression of anger and they are unjustly targeted by police more than other groups. To ignore such facts and engage in "generic" anger management skill development would be not only ineffective but also possibly harmful.

CONCLUSION: PUTTING THE PIECES TOGETHER

Building a Better Man is a science-based initiative grounded in the literature. It integrates elements that show evidence of efficacy and avoids those that have proven ineffective. Consistent with the literature, our initiative is a multicultural, Selected/Indicated, CBT, and socioecological prevention program that, through dialogue and skill building activities, addresses masculinity and identity, communication and discipline within the family, life skills development, alcohol and drug abuse, gender equality, social norms that promote violence, and issues of advocacy.

A central piece of our program is that we recognize that our society's definition of masculinity is limited and narrow, and leads to violence among males. Therefore, as presented through our Masculinity Developmental Hierarchy, males who increase their awareness of the impact that masculinity hegemony and mainstream socialization have on their notions of gender differences, gender roles, power, and use of force can make better choices, and accept greater responsibility for their role in society in creating and maintaining fairness and equality across genders.

The main goals of our initiative are to develop a strong and healthy sense of identity, decrease the use of violence, increase male engagement in the prevention of violence, increase community participation, and achieve liberation from oppressive societal constructions. Although our initiative incorporates multiple perspectives and approaches, we feel it is unique in its focus and process. Our hope is that our work will be adopted by other organizations and prevention advocates.

NOTES

1. World Health Organization (1996). *Violence: A public health priority*. Geneva: WHO Global Consultation on Violence and Health.

2. Butchart, A., Phinney, A., Check, P., & Villaveces, A. (2004). *Preventing violence: A guide to implementing the recommendations of the World Report on Violence and Health*. Geneva: Department of Injuries and Violence Prevention, World Health Organization.

3. Ibid.

4. Krug, E.G., Dahlberg, L.L., Mercy, J.A., Zwi, A.B., & Lozano, R. (2002). *World report on violence and health*. Geneva: World Health Organization. Retrieved from: http://www.who.int/violence_injury_prevention/violence/world_report/en/.

5. Krug et al. (2002). *World report on violence and health*.

6. Office of the Surgeon General, National Center for Injury Prevention and Control; National Institute of Mental Health; and Center for Mental Health Services (2001). *Youth violence: A report of the Surgeon General*. Rockville, MD: Office of the Surgeon General (US). Retrieved from: http://www.ncbi.nlm.nih.gov/books/NBK44294/.

7. Krug et al. (2002). *World report on violence and health*.

8. Ibid.

9. Ibid.

10. Ibid.

11. Ibid.

12. Department of Health and Human Services (2001). *Youth violence: A report of the Surgeon General*. Retrieved from: www.surgeongeneral.gov/library/youthviolence/toc.html.

13. Matjasko, J.L., Vivolo-Kantor, A.M., Massetti, G.M., Holland, K.M., Holt, M.K., & De la Cruz, J. (2012). A systematic meta-review of evaluations of youth violence prevention programs: Common and divergent findings from 25 years of meta-analyses and systematic reviews. *Aggression and Violent Behavior, 17(6)*, 540–552.

14. Bronfenbrenner, U. (1979). *The ecology of human development*. Cambridge, MA: Harvard University Press.

15. Department of Health and Human Services (2001). *Youth violence: A report of the Surgeon General*. Retrieved from: www.surgeongeneral.gov/library/youthviolence/toc.html.

    Lipsey, M.W. & Derzon, J.H. (1998). Predictors of violent and serious delinquency in adolescence and early adulthood: A synthesis of longitudinal research. In R. Loeber & D.P. Farrington (Eds.), *Serious and violent juvenile offenders: Risk factors and successful interventions* (pp. 86–105). Thousand Oaks, CA: Sage.

    Mercy, J., Butchart, A., Farrington, D., & Cerdá, M. (2002). Youth violence. In E. Krug, L.L. Dahlberg, J.A. Mercy, A.B. Zwi, & R. Lozano (Eds.), *World report on violence and health*. Geneva: World Health Organization. Retrieved from: http://www.who.int/violence_injury_prevention/violence/global_campaign/en/chap2.pdf.

    Resnick, M.D., Ireland, M., & Borowsky, I. (2004). Youth violence perpetration: what protects? What predicts? Findings from the National Longitudinal Study of Adolescent Health. *Journal of Adolescent Health, 35(424)*, e1–e10.

16. Vigil, J.D. & Yun, S.C. (2002). A cross-cultural framework to understand gangs: Multiple marginality and Los Angeles. In C.R. Huff (Ed.), *Gangs in America* (3rd ed., pp. 161–174). Thousand Oaks, CA: Sage.

17. Dutton, D.G. & Gorvo, K. (2006). Transforming a flawed policy: A call to revive psychology and science in domestic violence research and practice. *Aggression and Violent Behavior, 77(5)*, 457–483.

18. Labriola, M., Rempel, M., & Davis, R. (2005). Testing the effectiveness of batterer programs and judicial monitoring: Final report submitted to the

National Institute of Justice. Retrieved June 29, 2006, from: http://www. courtinnovation.org/_uploads/documents/battererprogramseffectiveness.pdf.

19. World Health Organization (2010). Violence prevention: The evidence. WHO Library Cataloguing-in-Publication Data. Retrieved from: http://apps.who. int/iris/bitstream/10665/77936/1/9789241500845_eng.pdf.
20. Ibid.
21. Matjasko et al. (2012). A systematic meta-review.
22. Krug et al. (2002). *World report on violence and health*.
23. Ibid.
24. Berkowitz, A. (2004). *Working with men to prevent violence: An overview (Part One)*. Harrisburg, PA: VAWnet, a project of the National Resource Center on Domestic Violence/Pennsylvania Coalition against Domestic Violence. Retrieved from: http://www.vawnet.org.
25. Ibid.
26. US Census Bureau (2011). Current population survey: Annual social and economic supplements. Retrieved from: http://www.census.gov/hhes/ www/poverty/publications/pubs-cps.html.
27. Russell, L. (2010). Easing the burden: Using health care reform to address racial and ethnic disparities in health care for the chronically ill. Center for American Progress. Retrieved from: www.americanprogress.org/issues/ 2010/12/pdf/chronic_disparities.pd.
28. Centers for Disease Control and Prevention (2011). National diabetes fact sheet: National estimates and general information on diabetes and prediabetes in the United States, 2011. Atlanta, GA: US Department of Health and Human Services, Centers for Disease Control and Prevention, 2011. Retrieved from: www.cdc.gov/diabetes/pubs/factsheet11.htm.
29. Centers for Disease Control and Prevention (2011). CDC health disparities and inequalities report—United States, 2011. MMWR. Retrieved from: www.cdc.gov/mmwr/pdf/other/su6001.pdf.
30. Schiller, J.S., Lucas, J.W., & Peregoy, J.A. (2012). Summary health statistics for U.S. adults: National Health Interview Survey, 2011. National Center for Health Statistics. Vital and Health Statistics Series 10(256).
31. National Cancer Institute (2009). Cancer statistics review, 1975–2006. Retrieved from: http://seer.cancer.gov/csr/1975_2006/results_single/sect_.
32. Centers for Disease Control and Prevention (2011). CDC health disparities and inequalities report—United States, 2011.
33. Ibid.
34. Ibid.
35. Azzam, A.M. (2008). Neglecting higher achievers. *Educational Leadership*, *66*, 90–92.
36. National Center for Education Statistics (2002). Education longitudinal study of 2002. Retrieved from http://nces.ed.gov/surveys/els2002/bibliography.asp.
37. US Census Bureau (2010). 2010 Census data products: United States. Retrieved from: http://www.census.gov/2010census/.
38. US Census Bureau (2011). Current population survey: Annual social and economic supplements. Retrieved from: http://www.census.gov/hhes/ www/poverty/publications/pubs-cps.html.
39. Ibid.
40. US Department of Labor (2011). The African-American Labor Force in the Recovery. Retrieved from: http://www.dol.gov/_sec/media/reports/black laborforce/.
41. Engel, R.S. & Calnon, J.M. (2004). Examining the influence of drivers' characteristics during traffic stops with the police: Results from a national survey. *Justice Quarterly, (21)1*, 49–90.

42. Spohn, C. (2001). Thirty years of sentencing reform: The quest for a racially neutral sentencing process. In W. Reed and L. Winterfield (Eds.). *Criminal Justice 2000* (Vol. 3, p. 566). Washington, DC: National Institute of Justice.
43. Guerino, P., Harrison, P.M., & Sabol, W.J. (2011). Prisoners in 2010. *Bulletin.* National Criminal Justice 236095. Washington, DC: United States Department of Justice, Bureau of Justice Statistics.
44. Ibid.
45. US Department of Health and Human Services, Office of Minority Health (2013). Enhanced National Standards for Culturally and Linguistically Appropriate Services in Health Care. Retrieved from http://www.omhrc. gov/clas/.
46. Cross, T., Bazron, B., Dennis, K., & Issacs, M. (1989). *Towards a culturally competent system of care: A monograph on effective services for minority children who are severely emotionally disturbed.* Washington, DC: CASPP Technical Assistance Center, Georgetown University Child Development Center.
47. Sue, D. & Sue, D. (2012). *Counseling the culturally diverse: Theory and practice* (6th ed.). Hoboken, NJ: John Wiley & Sons Inc.
48. Arciniega, G., Anderson, T.C., Tovar-Blank, Z.G., & Tracey, T.G. (2008). Toward a fuller conception of machismo: Development of a traditional machismo and caballerismo scale. *Journal of Counseling Psychology, 55(1),* 19–33.
49. Guerra, N.G. & Phillips-Smith, E. (2005). *Preventing youth violence in a multicultural society.* Washington, DC: American Psychological Association, doi: 10.1037/11380-000.
50. Gabbidon, S.L. & Greene, H.T. (Eds.) (2005). *Race, crime, and justice: A reader.* New York: Routledge.

CHAPTER 5

BUILDING A BETTER MAN GROUPS FOR MALES

The Building a Better Man group intervention focuses on three areas of improvement that we refer to as the three "I's"—Intrapersonal Awareness, Interpersonal Skills Training, and Community Involvement. The program is designed to *protect, educate, and connect* boys and men as they develop their own definition of masculinity, or help them alter it in a positive direction, whether they are at the Dependent Acquisition, Conscious Transformation, or Active Awareness levels. The following workbook curriculum for an eight-session group reflects this program emphasis and is representative of the type of groups we run through the Building a Better Man Project. This will serve as a guide to facilitators who would like to adopt it for use with the men and boys they work with. It is not meant to be rigid, but rather a template for facilitators who should make necessary adjustments to fit the desired needs, average ages, and personality of their groups. As all males and group dynamics are different, we believe it is not appropriate to advocate for a "cookie cutter" intervention that would presumably meet the varied needs of those involved in therapy or a psychoeducational group. The intent of this workbook is to provide opportunities for all males to learn the same essential skills (through *education*), but in a manner that resonates with them and promotes safe sharing of deeper-seated emotions (through *protection*) and opportunities to practice new ways-of-being (through *connection*).

The group sessions are based on the premise of "edutainment," being both educative and entertaining. We do not want these terms to be mutually exclusive, as the previous review of effective interventions would suggest that simply imparting information without participant involvement and interest is generally ineffective in promoting behavior change. Our goal for each session is to hold the attention of men (particularly young men) through dynamic discourse and the use of multimedia (such as YouTube clips, music, and other video) without sacrificing the integrity of the instruction to be delivered (i.e., adherence to cognitive-behavioral principles and therapeutic techniques). Each session begins with an "I" area of focus, a rationale for that focus, and the goal to be met. The session flow is likened to that of a concert experience, with an opening act (introduction), a headliner (the main activity), and an after party (homework).

Each session below provides options that can be used by the facilitator that fit the personality of the group. The purpose of these options is to help keep each session fresh and the participants interested, so that the goal of the session is accomplished.

One consistent element across sessions is the recitation of the group creed. Each session begins with the following affirmation:

> We believe in the power to shape our own destiny. We believe we hold limitless power in our hands. Our mission is to maximize our potential and positively share our gifts with the world.

The purpose of the creed is to help reinforce the notion that males have the ability through awareness, transformation, and action to change their behavior, which ties in with the premise of the Masculinity Developmental Hierarchy. A key concept in the creed is accountability. The participant understands that his own genuine input, buy-in, and confidence are the decisive elements that will predict the level of success he obtains in the program.

For those who are interested in formal assessment of progress, a quantitative assessment of masculinity ideologies, Levant et al.'s Male Role Norms Inventory (MRNI) and its subsequent adolescent version, the MRNI-A, could potentially be used in a pre/post manner to assess attitudinal change.[1] For young men, behavior change can also be assessed by a general measure such as the Behavior Assessment System for Children (BASC), which is available in self-report, parent, and teacher versions.[2] Other quantitative options include tracking disciplinary or incident referrals in school settings, or police contacts in the community pre/post. Qualitative assessment is based on participant feedback, specifically a letter-writing assignment (see below) designed to help each participant synthesize and operationalize what they learned about themselves and their notion of masculinity. Two examples of these letters are found in the Preface. For young men and boys, parents/caregivers also participate in an informal exit interview.

Note: The workbook describes the eight-session group curriculum and accompanying handouts. We also run 24-week Building a Better Man groups that allow for greater depth and breadth of coverage. However, the general curriculum and emphasis are the same. For purposes of this book, only the eight-session curriculum is included below.

NOTES

1. The Male Role Norms Inventory (MRNI) and Related Instruments. Retrieved from: http://www.drronaldlevant.com/mrni.html.
2. The Behavior Assessment System for Children-Second Edition (BASC-2). Retrieved from: http://www.pearsonclinical.com/psychology/products/100000658/behavior-assessment-system-for-children-second-edition-basc-2.html.

BUILDING A BETTER MAN

EIGHT-WEEK GROUP CURRICULUM FOR MALES

Area of Focus: Intrapersonal Awareness

- Session One: Manhood
- Session Two: Understanding Our Actions
- Session Three: Who Am I?
- Session Four: Where Am I Going?

Area of Focus: Interpersonal Skills Training

- Session Five: Understanding Challenging Social Interactions
- Session Six: Understanding Relationships with Others

Area of Focus: Community Involvement

- Session Seven: Connecting You to Your Community
- Session Eight: Staying Connected and Getting "Better"

SESSION ONE

Area of Focus: Intrapersonal Awareness
Topic: **Manhood**
Goals:

- To describe the purpose of the group
- To share guidelines, rules, and expectations
- To help improve intrapersonal awareness
- To personally define the meaning of the word "manhood"

Discussion Questions for this Session:

1. What do you expect from this group?
2. What messages have you received from society, media, family, and school about being a man?
3. How do you define manhood?
4. How do you know you have become a man?
5. What are characteristics that describe a "Superior Man" and an "Inferior Man?"
6. In what ways are you involved in your community?

Agenda:

I. Opening Act
   a. Introduction
   b. Group Overview
   c. Icebreaker
   d. Guidelines
   e. Creed
II. Headliner
   a. Manhood: The Superior Man vs. Inferior Man
III. After Party
   a. Random Acts of Kindness (RAK)
   b. Wisdom

SESSION ONE BREAKDOWN

I. Opening Act

   a. Introduction: The first session sets an enthusiastic tone that promotes participant buy-in. Introduce yourself in a manner that helps you join with the participants, such as revealing why you are facilitating the group and/or what your own experience of manhood has been. One option is to share a "fun" fact about you that participants would not have guessed and then ask them to do the same. For example, a facilitator could say, "Hi my name is Jay. At age fifteen I competed as part of a national soccer team. Now you tell me your name and a fun fact about yourself."

   b. Group Overview: After everyone does some initial sharing, take some time to describe the project and the long-term and short-term goals. At this time briefly describe the three I's and their importance to the work the group will be doing in the coming weeks. Here is one way of putting it:

      i. *Intrapersonal Awareness*: You cannot change yourself unless you know yourself. This requires the courage to look in the mirror and face what has been hidden.

      ii. *Interpersonal Skills Development*: You already know what gets you in trouble, but you may not know what doesn't. This requires learning and practicing new ways of acting.

      iii. *Community Involvement*: You are already involved in your community; you just need to decide whether that involvement will promote peace and harmony—or fear. This may require a shift from selfishness to selflessness.

   c. Icebreaker: Make sure the icebreaker is appropriate for the group in terms of age of participants, physical capabilities, etc. A good icebreaker promotes communication, group cohesion, and fun. There are a variety of icebreakers and low ropes activities by age/gender available on the internet. Select these with safety in mind as well.

   d. Guidelines: When discussing guidelines, make clear that it is important for groups to have order. However, it is perhaps counterproductive to spend much time on rules, as the participant group may be quite adept at breaking them. Hence, focus on "respect"—the need to respect yourself and others in the group by listening and participating. Consequences for disrespectful behavior are implied, but not delineated. The goal is to keep a positive focus in each session.

   e. Creed: The transition from the three I's and the respect rule to the creed is fairly seamless, as the tenets of the creed encapsulate all of these. The goal is for participants to begin verbalizing that they have some control of their situation, that they control their destiny and have the power to change, and that this power should be used positively to help themselves and others. The creed should be revisited throughout each session, and participants should know that it is to be committed to memory.

II. Headliner

    a. Manhood: The essence of this session involves building a definition of manhood and masculinity that is functional and healthy. Do this by exploring stereotypes, personal definitions, rites of passage (or lack of), and role models as outlined in the above discussion questions. Generally try to explore the unrealistic notion that men are dichotomous (e.g., good or bad, mature or immature, hero or villain), moving participants to an understanding that elements of both can coexist inside themselves. This sets up a discussion of the Superior Man vs. the Inferior Man. Note the positive aspects of manhood (as listed in the handout "Positive Aspects of Being a Male") that describe qualities that can be common to all men regardless of their status. However, the point must be clearly made that a Superior Man uses these qualities in a nonviolent and prosocial manner, whereas the Inferior Man does not. The Superior Man is not perfect, but he does learn from his mistakes. The Inferior Man does not. For example, a man can demonstrate courage and risk-taking, and band together with others, but this could describe either a fire-fighter or a gang-banger—and the outcomes for each depend on how they conduct themselves. The facilitator can also refer to the Masculinity Developmental Hierarchy (MDH) to further the discussion (see Chapter 3 and the MDH handout). The central message is that *you* have the power to decide how to use those attributes. This can lead to a discussion of how young men impact their communities—for good or ill, promoting either peace and harmony or generating fear. Regardless, young men *matter* and they are important to their families and communities.

III. After Party

    a. <u>Random Acts of Kindness (RAK)</u>: To begin to demonstrate the impact young men have on their families and communities, homework is assigned. Explain the concept of RAK as voluntarily doing something good for someone else. The RAK is a way to introduce and weave community involvement into each session. Initially, begin by asking each participant to do something good for a family member and then report to the group next time. Ask each participant to describe what he did, for whom, how that person reacted, and how that made the participant feel. For young men or boys, this can be introduced as a competition in which they can earn "RAK points" that lead to a reward by the end of the eight weeks. Progressive RAK assignments move from the family to the neighborhood/school to the larger community across the eight sessions.

    b. <u>Wisdom</u>: The second assignment is to have participants find quotes, lyrics, video clips, or other media that resonate with them and depict struggle, common experiences, and/or positive qualities in men. These are shared with the group at the next session. For the first week the search would be related to the topic of manhood.

SESSION ONE HANDOUTS

THE MASCULINITY DEVELOPMENTAL HIERARCHY (MDH)

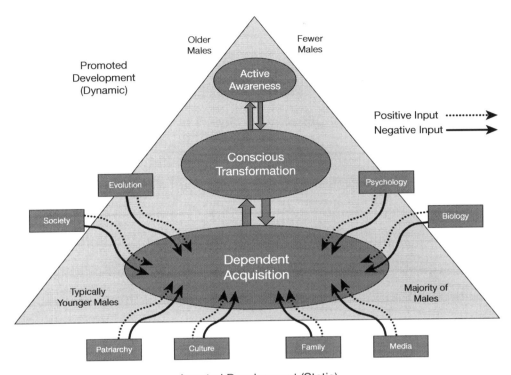

POSITIVE ASPECTS OF BEING A MALE

You are on your way to becoming a role model if you . . .

Relate to others by creating friendships through shared activities

Express care by protecting the innocent, taking action, and expressing emotion

Pass on fathering skills to sons and daughters

Are self-reliant, considering the input of others, resisting coercion, and sticking with a decision

Go to work, providing for your family, and taking pride in this

Demonstrate courage and risk-taking but distinguish between sensible and foolish risks

Band together to achieve a common goal

Contribute to the common good through volunteering and random acts of kindness

Use humor through good-natured ribbing

Are heroic in how you lead your life, using all of the above

This isn't a complete list, so there may be more of these for you as an individual . . .

SESSION TWO

Area of Focus: Intrapersonal Awareness
Topic: Understanding Our Actions
Goal:

- To explore how we think and the emotional/behavioral consequences of our thoughts

Discussion Questions for this Session:

1. What is the thinking cycle? Give examples of how this works.
2. What are antecedents?
3. What is the RACE Strategy?
4. What is the purpose of an Emotions Log?

Agenda:

I. Opening Act
   a. Group Creed
   b. Review Last Session
   c. Icebreaker (Introduction to the Tie)
   d. RAK and Wisdom
II. Headliner
   a. The Thinking Cycle
   b. The RACE Strategy
III. After Party
   a. Introduce the Morning Meditation and Nightly Reflection
   b. RAK
   c. Wisdom

SESSION TWO BREAKDOWN

I. Opening Act

    a. <u>The Creed</u>: The session begins with the group reciting and discussing the creed.

    b. <u>Session Review</u>: Review the last session. An engaging way to do this with young men is by tossing a ball around and asking participants to say something about the previous session when they catch it.

    c. <u>Icebreaker—Introduction to the Tie (young men and boys)</u>: The opening exercise today is the ritual of formally tying a tie. Many young males don't know how to do this, so they typically seem to appreciate the instruction. The activity serves multiple purposes, including relationship-building with the facilitator, completing a small rite of passage, and encouraging group cohesion through helping each other. Repeat this activity periodically in follow-on sessions. See the handout.

    d. <u>RAK and Wisdom</u>: Encourage participants to share their RAK activities and wisdom. Record points if a competition.

II. Headliner

    a. <u>The Thinking Cycle</u>: The main discussion for this session involves understanding the basics of cognitive-behavioral theory. The participants are familiarized with the Antecedent-Behavior-Consequence (A-B-C) sequence and how it fits into the "thinking cycle." See the handout. This discussion is an important one as follow-on sessions will continuously refer to these concepts and they are also aligned with the creed. Here are the critical components:

        i. **A**ntecedent: An event that triggers a reaction. It can come in the form of a direct positive or negative experience (e.g., a compliment or a verbal/physical attack) or an indirect one (e.g., you observe something happening). The trigger sets in motion a cycle of reaction.

        ii. Thinking: As human beings, our brains produce instantaneous thoughts about the triggering event. It is important to note that thoughts are easiest to change. Let the participants know it is their thinking that *drives* emotion and behavior.

        iii. Feelings: Emphasize the importance of understanding our emotional responses and how they can be our friend or enemy (e.g., in men, sadness can often be masked as anger).

        iv. **B**ehavior: Discuss how thinking and emotions lead to a behavioral reaction, and that this can often be a lightning fast, impulsive process. The decision to act may or may not be conscious, but it is important to know how to slow it down and analyze it.

        v. **C**onsequence: Emphasize that it is important to assess how our decisions lead to either positive or negative consequences in life. Logically, a positive outcome should encourage a person to continue what they are doing. Conversely, a negative outcome should encourage a change in decision making and behavior. For many males, this can often be harder than it sounds because there are so many internal and external influences that conspire to make change difficult. Introduce the Emotions Log (see the handout) as a way to analyze where errors began (particularly in thinking) and develop alternatives that may lead to better outcomes when future triggering events occur.

    b. <u>The RACE Strategy</u>: To help emphasize the importance of reframing thoughts, introduce the RACE Strategy. See the handout. Note that our thinking influences our status as either a Superior or Inferior Man. Use the analogy of a race in which two competing reactions vie for dominance inside us: the superior reaction is more methodical and deliberate, while the inferior one is impulsive and operates on reflex. While the superior reaction does not guarantee a perfect outcome, it certainly will foster a positive one. Use the RACE acronym to help reinforce this superior-type of process:

        i. <u>R</u>ecognize the antecedent that has happened.

        ii. <u>A</u> Couple of Choices are generated that respond to the antecedent. The range of thinking will be from negative and destructive to positive and effective.

        iii. <u>C</u>hoose the Best One that will produce a positive result.

        iv. <u>E</u>xecute that best choice.

III. After Party

    a. <u>Morning Meditation and Nightly Reflection Journal</u>: Introduce this mindfulness activity that helps participants be more aware of their daily goals, activities, and reactions. See the handout.

    b. <u>RAK</u>: Ask each participant to continue to do something good for a family member and then report to the group next time. Ask each participant to describe what he did, for whom, how that person reacted, and how that made the participant feel.

    c. <u>Wisdom</u>: This week's collected wisdom will be related to choices, mistakes, decision-making, and problem solving.

SESSION TWO HANDOUTS

THE HALF-WINDSOR NECKTIE KNOT

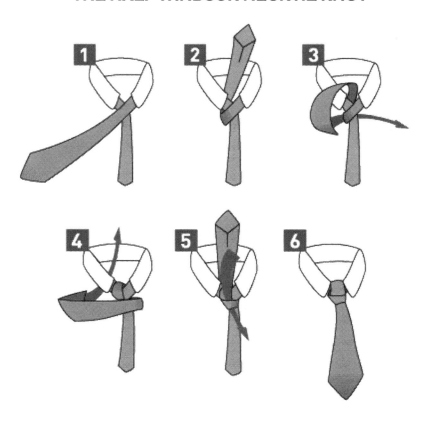

THE FOUR IN HAND NECKTIE KNOT

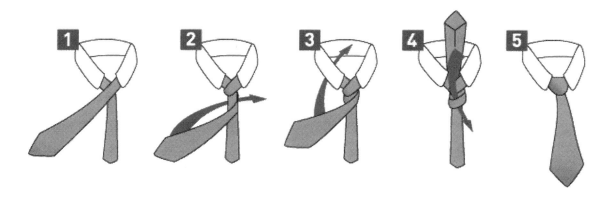

Images courtesy of Bows-N-Ties, 80 Langton Street, 1st Floor, San Francisco, CA, 94103

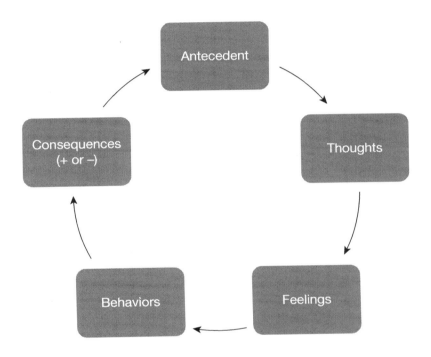

SESSION TWO HANDOUTS

THE RACE STRATEGY

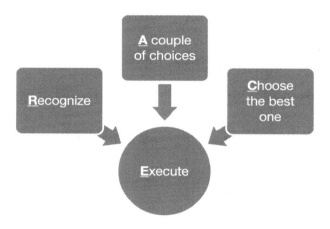

EMOTIONS LOG

Name: _____ Date: _____ Time: _____

What Emotions Did I Have?   Angry   Happy   Sad   Afraid   Anxious   Other:

_____

What Happened? _____

_____

Why Did This Happen? _____

_____

_____

What Was the Antecedent? _____

_____

_____

What Are Possible Solutions (Alternative Ways of Thinking about the

Antecedent)? _____

_____

_____

_____

_____

_____

_____

What Did I Learn from the Situation? _____

_____

_____

_____

What Will I Do Different Next Time? _____

_____

_____

_____

Will My Chosen Solution Work?   Yes   No

© William Seymour, Ramel Smith, and Héctor Torres, *Building a Better Man*, Routledge 2014

SESSION TWO HANDOUTS

MORNING MEDITATION

Date: _____

What are my goals for improving myself, helping others, and impacting my community positively today?

_____

_____

_____

Recite Your Personal Mantra or the Group Creed
Meditate/Pray on These Objectives:

1. Improve myself in mind, body, and soul
2. Help my family and friends
3. Impact my neighborhood and community positively

Date: _____

What are my goals for improving myself, helping others, and impacting my community positively today?

_____

_____

_____

Recite Your Personal Mantra or the Group Creed

Meditate/Pray on These Objectives:

1. Improve myself in mind, body, and soul
2. Help my family and friends
3. Impact my neighborhood and community positively

SESSION TWO HANDOUTS

NIGHTLY REFLECTION

Reflect on your Day . . .

I met my goals for:

• Improvement of Self

Strongly Agree	Agree	Neutral	Disagree	Strongly Disagree
1	2	3	4	5

• Helping Others

Strongly Agree	Agree	Neutral	Disagree	Strongly Disagree
1	2	3	4	5

• Impacting My Community Positively

Strongly Agree	Agree	Neutral	Disagree	Strongly Disagree
1	2	3	4	5

My overall grade for myself would be

A	B	C	D	F	Incomplete

What did I do well today?

_____

_____

_____

What could I do better tomorrow?

_____

_____

_____

Recite Your Personal Mantra or the Group Creed:

SESSION THREE

Area of Focus: Intrapersonal Awareness
Topic: Who Am I?
Goal: To develop an in-depth knowledge of self

Discussion Questions for this Session:

1. What are your personal strengths and weaknesses?
2. Is it acceptable for a man to cry?
3. What are some emotions that as men we try to ignore?
4. Is everything that happens to you a test of your manhood?
5. Can you make mistakes or try something new and be okay with the result?

Agenda:

I. Opening Act
    a. Group Creed
    b. Review Last Session
    c. Icebreaker
    d. Emotions Log, RAK, and Wisdom

II. Headliner
    a. Pyramid of Self-Knowledge
    b. Old and New Emotions
    c. SWOT Analysis
    d. Coat of Arms

III. After Party
    a. Emotions Log, Meditation, and Reflection
    b. RAK
    c. Wisdom

SESSION THREE BREAKDOWN

I. Opening Act

   a. Group Creed.

   b. Review Last Session.

   c. Icebreaker: Practice with ties or do another activity.

   d. Emotions Log, RAK, and Wisdom: Encourage participants to share their logs, RAK activities, and wisdom. Record points if a competition.

II. Headliner

   a. <u>Pyramid of Self-Knowledge</u>: The goal here is to truly focus on knowledge of self. It is important that males understand their relative strengths and weaknesses, and the forces that shape their character and actions so that they know what to change. Refer back to the Masculinity Developmental Hierarchy (MDH) to illustrate this. For participants' purposes, the MDH can be thought of more simply as a "Pyramid of Self-Knowledge" (see handout), which can aid them in listing the external and internal influences in their lives. The bottom level includes things that shape ***who you are*** (basic skills, traits, virtues, and vices) and that either promote their development as men or arrest it. Ask them to think about the influences around them that do this (e.g., family, friends, community, media, and discrimination). The middle level describes ***how you could be better*** by making some key changes (e.g., avoiding negative family members or friends, gaining more education, and deciding to rely less on societal reinforcement for maintaining a narrow definition of masculinity). The highest level is reserved for a description of ***who you want to be*** (e.g., incorporating traits of male role models known personally or through the culture, maintaining a broadened view of masculinity, and staying the course despite limited reinforcement for this new view). It may also be useful for the participants to refer back to the Positive Aspects of Being a Male handout to complete this activity.

   b. <u>Old and New Emotions</u>: Talk about "old" versus "new" emotions. As men we are taught to be unemotional, but being angry is okay. What about those other emotions that we try to ignore but we still have . . . like fear, shame, sadness, and worry? What about crying? Challenge the participants that if they are "man enough" and secure with themselves, they can try on these new emotions and see what they feel like without worrying that they are less of a man, or a failure as a man, or that they have failed some kind of manhood test. It may be useful to discuss shame and how it affects males. Point out that, as men, we may be embarrassed by feeling vulnerable or needing connection, and the shame we experience as a result can take its toll on us. Also explore how shame is used in such things as sports, the military, and business to motivate individual males to "act like a man!"

   c. <u>SWOT Analysis</u>: To further the goal of increased self-knowledge for the participants, an example from the business world is helpful. Discuss how before business owners invest in a new market or product line, they will conduct a Strengths–Weaknesses–Opportunities–Threats (SWOT)

analysis. This feasibility-type study allows for important decision making based on a comparison of the strengths and weaknesses of their business plan, and the perceived opportunities and threats involved. For the participants, bill this as essentially the "Business of YOU!" and have them complete the activity based on a major change they may be contemplating. See the handout.

    d. <u>Coat of Arms</u>: This activity can be used to further define for the participants their identity in positive terms. The Coat of Arms has its origin in medieval times in which knights decorated their shields to protect and identify themselves, each design being unique to their family of origin and representative of their own individual strengths. The knight analogy is useful to group participants as it serves as a reminder of what they aspire to be; that is, men of strength and honor. The Coat of Arms activity also ties in nicely with the notion of the Superior Man, the creed, and the three "I's." Have participants complete this task using the handout that describes what each of the four quadrants represents.

III. After Party

    a. <u>Emotions Log, Meditations, and Reflections</u>: Remind participants to complete these daily.

    b. <u>RAK</u>: Ask each participant to continue to do something good for a family member, but also expand this to people in the neighborhood. Report to the group next time. Ask each participant to describe what he did, for whom, how that person reacted, and how that made the participant feel.

    c. <u>Wisdom</u>: This week's collected wisdom will be related to recognizing and acknowledging personal strengths/weaknesses, and challenging oneself to try new things.

SESSION THREE HANDOUTS

PYRAMID OF SELF-KNOWLEDGE

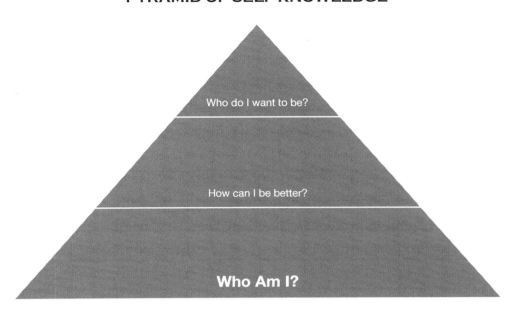

Who am I (skills, traits, virtues, vices)?

_____

_____

_____

_____

How can I be better (key changes I could make in my life)?

_____

_____

_____

_____

Who do I want to be (think about male role models)?

_____

_____

_____

_____

SWOT ANALYSIS

What is my "business plan" for change?

_____

_____

_____

_____

Complete the table below to see if this change is feasible.

Strengths	*Weaknesses*
Opportunities	*Threats*

Based on the above, can I do it?   Yes   No

COAT OF ARMS

If you were to design a Coat of Arms for yourself, what would it look like? Use the shield below to illustrate this in words, pictures, or both. Each quadrant can represent a personal or family strength, an important event in your life, an admired role model, or a strongly held belief.

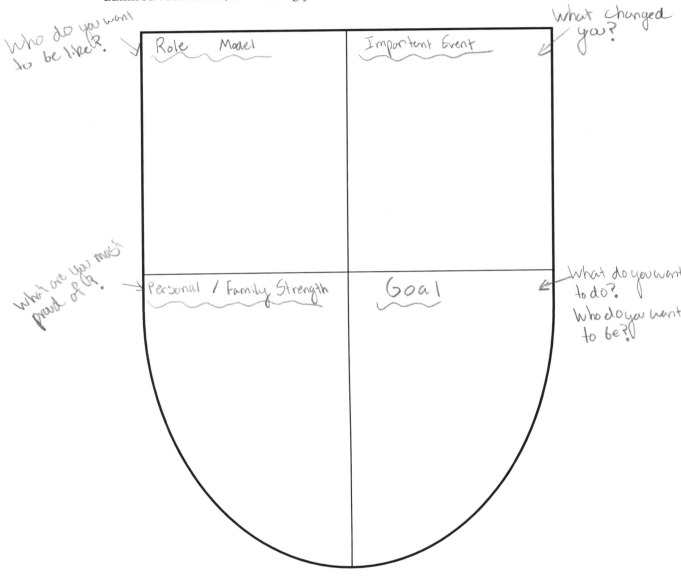

Who do you want to be like?

What changed you?

Role Model

Important Event

What are you most proud of?

Personal / Family Strength

Goal

What do you want to do?

Who do you want to be?

SESSION FOUR

Area of Focus: Intrapersonal Awareness
Topic: Where Am I Going?
Goals:

- To understand the importance of setting goals
- To learn how to form, monitor, and evaluate goals

Discussion Questions for this Session:

1. In what ways do goals benefit you?
2. How can you determine if a chosen goal fits you?
3. How do you know you have achieved your goal?

Agenda:

I. Opening Act
   a. Group Creed
   b. Review Last Session
   c. Icebreaker
   d. Emotions Log, RAK, and Wisdom
II. Headliner
   a. Goal Setting
III. After Party
   a. The Vision Board
   b. Emotions Log
   c. RAK
   d. Wisdom

SESSION FOUR BREAKDOWN

I. Opening Act

    a. Group Creed.

    b. Review Last Session.

    c. Icebreaker: Practice with ties or do another activity.

    d. Emotions Log, RAK, and Wisdom: Encourage participants to share their logs, RAK activities, and wisdom. Record points if a competition.

II. Headliner

    a. <u>Goal Setting</u>: Emphasize to the participants that self-awareness usually results in a decision either to change or to stay the same. If it is determined that personal change is necessary and desirable, goal setting will be critical to a successful outcome. Goals help us quantify what it is we want to achieve. Otherwise, it will be difficult to know how to proceed, how to measure progress, and when to declare victory. Goals also help remind us to stay the course, and how to adjust things if no progress is being made. Ask the participants to form two or three "better man" goals for their lives using the handout. Ask them to look at the MDH handout and determine what goals will help them promote their own development. These can be short term (e.g., days or weeks) or long term (e.g., years). Help them understand that it is important to choose an attainable goal, one that is challenging but not impossible; and that measurable benchmarks (objectives) will help them gauge progress toward a goal. Consider the following motivational definitions as a starting point for participant goal setting:

        i. ***Vision:*** *The ability to see. Something that you imagine. The act or power of anticipating that which will or may come to be.* The participant is reminded of the creed's "destiny" and "limitless power" references.

        ii. ***Envision:*** *To picture in the mind; imagine. To conceive of as a possibility, especially in the future; foresee.* Inspires the participant to dream big and create a plan to make these dreams reality.

        iii. ***Provision:*** *Something that is done in advance to prepare for something else. The act or process of supplying or providing something.* The participant understands what he needs in terms of effort, resources, and time to make his plan realistic.

        iv. ***Supervision:*** *The action or process of watching and directing what someone does or how something is done.* The participant monitors his own progress with measurable benchmarks and target dates for their completion. This builds momentum and stacks successes.

        v. ***Revision:*** *A revised or new version. A change or a set of changes that corrects or improves something. A new version of something.* The participant continuously assesses progress and revises benchmarks and target dates based on that assessment.

    b. <u>The Vision Board</u>: Similar to the SWOT analysis, this exercise helps the participants identify variables (e.g., persons or situations) that contribute to or detract from goal completion, using as a reference mathematical symbols as follows:

   i. Multiplication: Variables that can *directly help assist you.*

   ii. Addition: Variables that cannot help directly, but are *positive resources available for support.*

   iii. Subtraction: Variables that *unintentionally hinder you* from obtaining your goal.

   iv. Division: Variables that *actively conspire to plot your failure or present barriers to success.*

III. After Party

   a. <u>Goal Setting and the Vision Board</u>: Start this in session and complete it as homework if needed.

   b. <u>Emotions Log, Meditations, and Reflections</u>: Remind participants to complete these daily.

   c. <u>RAK</u>: Ask each participant to continue to do something good for a family member and people in the neighborhood. Report to the group next time. Ask each participant to describe what he did, for whom, how that person reacted, and how that made the participant feel.

   d. <u>Wisdom</u>: This week's collected wisdom will be related to recognizing and acknowledging personal strengths/weaknesses, and challenging oneself to try new things.

SESSION FOUR HANDOUTS

GOAL SETTING

Personal "Better Man" Vision Statement:

_____

_____

How do I realize my vision?

Goal Number _____:

_____

_____

Specific Objective (measurable and time limited):

_____

_____

_____

Specific Objective (measurable and time limited):

_____

_____

_____

Specific Objective (measurable and time limited):

_____

_____

_____

How do I know when I have met my goal?

_____

_____

(Use copies of this handout to create additional goals)

THE VISION BOARD

List the people and situations in your life that either help you or hinder you from being a better man.

Multiplication (×): *Directly help you*	Addition (+): *Positive resources that you can draw on*	Subtraction (−): *Unintentionally hinder you*	Division (÷): *Actively conspire against you*

SESSION FIVE

Area of Focus: Interpersonal Skills Training
Topic: Understanding Challenging Social Interactions
Goals:

- To learn and practice positively assertive social skills
- To understand the concepts of social responsibility and citizenship

Discussion Questions for this Session:

1. Why are males disproportionately affected by violence?
2. How effective and positive are your interactions with others?
3. Is there a way to be positively assertive but not negatively aggressive when challenged by others?
4. How are all of us connected?
5. What does the term citizenship imply?
6. What are our personal responsibilities within our larger community?

Agenda:

I. Opening Act
    a. Group Creed
    b. Review Last Session
    c. Icebreaker
    d. Emotions Log, RAK, and Wisdom
II. Headliner
    a. Positively Assertive Social Skills (PASS)
    b. Bullying
III. After Party
    a. Emotions Log
    b. RAK
    c. Wisdom

SESSION FIVE BREAKDOWN

I. Opening Act

    a. Group Creed.

    b. Review Last Session.

    c. Icebreaker: Practice with ties or do another activity.

    d. Emotions Log, RAK, and Wisdom: Encourage participants to share their logs, RAK activities, and wisdom. Record points if a competition.

II. Headliner

    a. <u>Positively Assertive Social Skills (PASS)</u>: Discuss with participants that males are more likely to be victims and perpetrators of violence. The focus of this session is to learn how to avoid confrontation and violence in social interactions, particularly those that involve a perceived challenge to masculine "toughness" (e.g., responding to a derogatory comment, accepting an invitation to fight). For many of our young men, their environments dictate an aggressive response to provocation; hence, it is unrealistic to ask that they always avoid a fight. However, there is a "middle ground" response that is neither too weak (victimizing) nor too aggressive (confrontational). Refer to this as "positively assertive," meaning that there is a way to handle these challenges that does not lead to either victimization or a guaranteed physical fight. Refer back to the cognitive-behavioral teaching in Session Two that emphasizes the need to correctly interpret a perceived challenge (i.e., a perceived challenge to masculine toughness may actually be something else). If that analysis does result in the correct assumption that you are being challenged by another, then it is time to respond. Refer to the Challenge and Response Decision Tree below to help guide participants through this PASS process. As the tree indicates, there are direct and indirect ways to handle a challenge. The indirect route involves such strategies as avoidance, ignoring, deflecting, retreating, and seeking help. In situations in which an indirect response will not work (e.g., you are physically cornered by an assailant), a direct response is indicated. The direct response involves a defensive physical stance and assertive language use (e.g., "Don't do that to me" or "Let me pass"). If these things do not work, then a physical self-defense approach may be needed. For this session, a guest trainer is useful in teaching these self-defense skills to the participants. Throughout the discussion, use best-practice social skills training methods that are presented in a step-by-step manner. See the handout.

    b. <u>Bullying</u>: This is particularly applicable for boys and young men. The issue of bullying has been a long-standing problem; however, as of late it has received more societal attention because of the immediate and lethal consequences of the problem. Most young males have been familiarized with this problem through bullying education in the schools. Hence, a brief overview of the important points from this education is appropriate. However, emphasize that the positively assertive response above is certainly applicable to bullying. Also refer back to the Superior Man idea and the Positive Aspects of Being a Male discussion. Focus on the following points:

i. *Definition*: Bullying is aggressive behavior that is intended to cause harm or distress, occurs repeatedly over time, and occurs in a relationship in which there is an imbalance of power.

ii. *Discuss the bully triangle*:
1. Bully: The aggressor.
2. Victim: The individual or group that is targeted by the bully.
3. Bystander: A witness to the act. There are three types:
    1. Negative: Encourages and supports the action of the bully.
    2. Neutral: Neither encourages nor helps.
    3. Positive: Actively helps the victim by stopping the action, getting help, or providing care for the victim in the aftermath of the event. An individual or a group.

iii. *Discuss ways to bully*:
1. Physical: hitting, punching, kicking, pushing, spitting.
2. Emotional: socially isolating, verbally harassing, intimidating through the threat of physical force.
3. Cyber: social media, e-mailing, texting.

iv. *Discuss why people bully and the consequences of this for all involved*: It is likely that most of the participants have played all three roles in the triangle. Use personal examples and consequences to illustrate this. Note that long-term emotional and behavioral consequences exist for all three roles.

v. *Discuss interventions*:
1. School and community policies and laws
2. Prevention programs
3. Encourage the participants to make a personal commitment to be assertive as a target, positive as a bystander, and never an aggressor.

III. After Party

a. <u>Positively Assertive Social Skills (PASS)</u>: Remind participants to practice these during the week.

b. <u>Emotions Log, Meditations, and Reflections</u>: Remind participants to complete these daily.

c. <u>RAK</u>: Ask each participant to continue to do something good for a family member and people in the neighborhood. Report to the group next time. Ask each participant to describe what he did, for whom, how that person reacted, and how that made the participant feel.

d. <u>Wisdom</u>: This week's collected wisdom will be related to challenging oneself to try new things, moral courage, and helping others.

SESSION FIVE HANDOUTS

CHALLENGE AND RESPONSE DECISION TREE

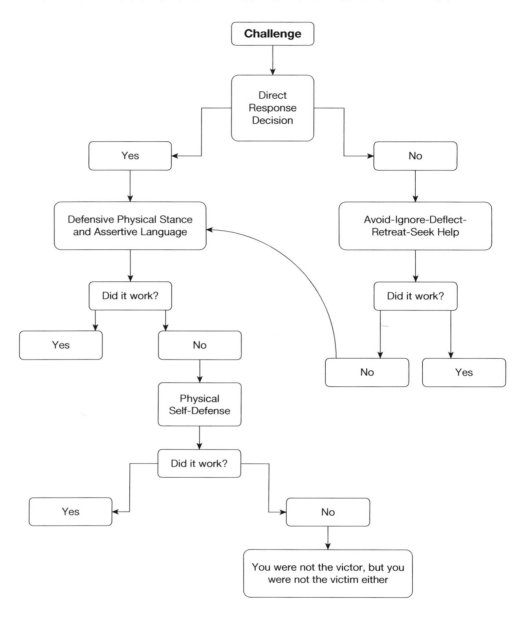

SESSION FIVE HANDOUTS

SOCIAL SKILLS TRAINING METHOD

Step 1:
<u>Introduce the Skill</u>: Provide a description and examples of when the skill would be appropriate to use.

Step 2:
<u>Provide a Rationale as to Why the Skill Is Important</u>: This relates back to the mantra from Session One: "You already know what gets you in trouble, but you may not know what doesn't. This requires learning and practicing new ways of acting." Also emphasize that any social skill intended to reduce violence, and therefore the likelihood of injury or death, is important to everyone.

Step 3:
<u>Demonstrate the Skill</u>: Model the behavior using volunteer participants. A guest trainer is appropriate for this purpose (e.g., a self-defense expert).

Step 4:
<u>Rehearse the Skill with Participants</u>: Have all participants actively practice the skill. Provide prompts, cues, coaching, and feedback.

Step 5:
<u>Provide Positive Reinforcement</u>: Praise participants for their work and comment on specific observations you made during the rehearsal.

Step 6:
<u>Encourage Generalization</u>: Suggest to participants that they try the new skill in their lives outside of session. Assign this as homework and praise/reward participants when they provide examples of how it worked for them.

SESSION SIX

Area of Focus: Interpersonal Skills Training
Topic: Understanding Relationships with Others
Goals:

- To help understand how relationships develop, evolve, dissolve, and resolve
- To understand male privilege and patriarchy, as well as biases based on gender and sexual orientation

Discussion Questions for this Session:

1. How do we distinguish between relationships that we need and those that we don't?
2. What are some ways that you benefit from how others treat you?
3. What are your responsibilities as a male in a relationship with someone else?
4. What is male privilege and how does it affect us?
5. What is patriarchy and how does it affect us?
6. How do you define sexism, heterosexism, and homophobia?

Agenda:

I. Opening Act
   a. Group Creed
   b. Review Last Session
   c. Icebreaker
   d. Emotions Log, RAK, and Wisdom
II. Headliner
   a. Relationships
   b. Male Privilege
III. After Party
   a. Five Friend Assessment
   b. PASS
   c. Emotions Log
   d. RAK
   e. Wisdom

SESSION SIX BREAKDOWN

I. Opening Act

    a. Group Creed.

    b. Review Last Session.

    c. Icebreaker: Practice with ties or do another activity.

    d. PASS, Emotions Log, RAK, and Wisdom: Encourage participants to share their PASS practice, logs, RAK activities, and wisdom. Record points if a competition.

II. Headliner

    a. <u>Relationships</u>: The focus of this session is on helping participants understand interpersonal relationships (e.g., friendship, romantic, work-related), the phases of relationships, and how to navigate through them effectively. Refer back to the difficulties many men have in opening themselves to others, being vulnerable, and trusting. Ultimately, these things are necessary in order to form deeper, intimate relationships. Discuss the notion that men should be *"tough, stoic, possessive, and self-reliant"* and how this inhibits our interactions with others. Then discuss the relationship phases as follows:

        i. *Introducing (Developing)*: Meeting new people through proximity with others such as family members, friends, and associates in places like neighborhoods, schools, sports teams, organizations, and faith sites. Discuss conversation skills, including introducing yourself, talking, listening, and ending interactions.

        ii. *Increasing (Evolving)*: With increased familiarity, divulging more detail about yourself, assessing the other's trustworthiness and integrity, taking relationship risks, and having the courage to be vulnerable.

        iii. *Ending (Devolving)*: In the natural course of lives, this can happen. There are positive endings (e.g., graduation, a new job, marriage, a move) and negative endings (e.g., sudden or gradual lack of contact, divorce, death, military deployment, incarceration). Discuss how some men have difficulty letting go because of possessiveness, fear, and shame. Refer back to accurately analyzing thoughts through the cognitive-behavioral process.

        iv. *Re-introducing (Resolving)*: It is possible that relationships may be re-established after a negative or positive ending. If the ending was negative, it is useful to analyze why the relationship failed initially, and the nature of the re-introduction. Discuss how to interpret this and assess how healthy the re-introduction may or may not be.

    Use the Five Friend Assessment activity in the handouts to help the participants further assess the nature of their relationships, including positive and negative qualities of the people they know, and then assess what these relationships say about them in terms of being better men. Refer back to the Vision Board activity as well.

b. <u>Male Privilege</u>: Discuss the notion that males enjoy privilege, often based solely on their gender and heterosexual status, and that this is maintained through a patriarchal system. This is particularly true for White males in the United States. Define patriarchy as *control by men of a disproportionately large share of power*. Membership in any dominant group provides an opportunity to think myopically, act exclusively, and abuse power, particularly if that group's membership is defined by aggression, competition, and acquisition. Discuss how it may be anxiety-provoking for any dominant group to relinquish power and privilege, particularly males. Privilege may be derived from a sense of entitlement, given that men generally assign themselves dangerous societal tasks such as soldiering and (potentially) providing. Discuss that White male dominance will decrease as demographic changes occur. More women are entering the workforce at the same time as minority groups gain more representative and economic power through population increases. Discuss how (White) men may respond to this inevitability. Also define as a group what "sexism," "heterosexism," and "homophobia" are. Ask participants to identify instances in which they themselves or others have been involved in a situation related to these biases (e.g., deriding a male's masculine status by denouncing him as "gay"). Process the consequences and the impact of these biases, and connect the discussion to power and patriarchy in our society. Have the participants complete the Beliefs and Biases Self-Assessment. See the handout.

III. After Party

a. <u>Five Friend Assessment</u>: Start this in session and complete it as homework if needed.

b. <u>Beliefs and Biases Self-Assessment</u>: Start this in session and complete it as homework if needed.

c. <u>Emotions Log, Meditations, and Reflections</u>: Remind participants to complete these daily.

d. <u>RAK</u>: Ask each participant to continue to do something good for a family member, people in the neighborhood, and now the community (e.g., public spaces, the workplace, or school). Report to the group next time. Ask each participant to describe what he did, for whom, how that person reacted, and how that made the participant feel.

e. <u>Wisdom</u>: This week's collected wisdom will be related to men and their interactions with others, intimacy, privilege, and overcoming biases.

SESSION SIX HANDOUTS

FIVE FRIEND ASSESSMENT

"You are the average of the five people you spend the most time with."
Jim Rohn, Business Philosopher

Name five friends/people you spend the most time with. Name two positives and one negative about them.

Friend:
- Two Positives:
- One Negative:

Friend:
- Two Positives:
- One Negative:

Friend:
- Two Positives:
- One Negative:

Friend:
- Two Positives:
- One Negative:

Friend:
- Two Positives:
- One Negative:

What do these relationships say about who you are as a man?

_____

_____

_____

SESSION SIX HANDOUTS

BELIEFS AND BIASES SELF-ASSESSMENT

Answer the questions below.

What helped you create your definition of masculinity?

_____

_____

How were you taught to view women by your family, culture, society, and the media?

_____

_____

How were you taught to view homosexuality by your family, culture, society, and the media?

_____

_____

How were you taught to interact with members of other races by your family, culture, society, and the media?

_____

_____

How have your life experiences and education challenged (or supported) your original views on all of these topics (i.e., masculinity, gender, sexual orientation, and race)?

_____

_____

What biases or views on these topics continue to limit your growth as a man? How do you know?

_____

_____

What is your plan to reduce biases you may have about others?

_____

_____

_____

_____

SESSION SEVEN

Area of Focus: Community Involvement
Topic: Connecting You to Your Community
Goals:

- Establish the connection between personal involvement and the health of the community
- Connect intrapersonal awareness and interpersonal skills to community involvement

Discussion Questions for this Session:

1. What is your role as a young man in your community?
2. Are you important to your community?
3. How does helping others help you?
4. How do you decide how much to "give back"?

Agenda:

I. Opening Act
   a. Group Creed
   b. Review Last Session
   c. Extended Sharing
II. Headliner
   a. Your Role in Your Community
   b. Group Project
III. After Party
   a. Building a Better Man Letter
   b. Group Project
   c. PASS
   d. Emotions Log
   e. RAK
   f. Wisdom

SESSION SEVEN BREAKDOWN

I.   Opening Act

    a.   Group Creed.

    b.   Review Last Session.

    c.   Extended Sharing: Encourage participants to share any of their activities and discoveries based on any of the assignments. Take extra time as there should be much to discuss at this point in the curriculum.

II. Headliner

    a.   <u>Your Role in Your Community</u>: The essential point for participants is that they *do* matter to their communities, whether as a Superior Man or an Inferior Man. In fact, it can be argued that young men set the tone for a neighborhood or community by their behavior—by the way they choose to conduct themselves. Use the Superior Man reference in this discussion as it is central to helping the participants see this. Ask them to envision a scenario in which all the young men in their communities are superior, and then the opposite. It is likely there will be stark contrasts, and that the inferior scenario may be closer to actual reality in some communities, where fear, distrust, and violence prevail. At this point, help them to understand that if one hypothetical scenario is reality, the other can easily be as well. Tie into this discussion intrapersonal awareness, interpersonal skills, and the creed. Review these and emphasize the fact that change in a community happens one person at a time, and that they have a significant stake in that.

    b.   <u>Group Project</u>: The group project should tie in as much of the above discussion as possible. It is a culminating activity that can create a sense of accomplishment and optimism. Let the group decide what to do, but be available to help and remind them that, ultimately, they are the agents of change with regard to decreasing violence and increasing prosocial behavior in themselves and their communities. Give the participants as much access to multimedia as possible to complete the project. The following are some ideas and possible options for the group:

       • Create a Public Service Announcement (PSA) on violence, bullying, or other relevant topics.

       • Create a video that has a "real talk" feel to it (i.e., men talking to other men).

       • Create a hypothetical Building a Better Man community organization.

       • Create a trailer for a movie that spreads a positive message about nonviolence.

       • Create a collection of lyrics, raps, poems, quotes, proverbs, and axioms that have been brought to the group throughout the previous sessions.

       • Create a social media page that fosters awareness about a relevant topic.

       • Organize as a group and agree to volunteer time to a worthy organization in the community (e.g., Habitat for Humanity).

III. After Party

    a. <u>Building a Better Man Letter</u>: Start this in session and complete it as homework if needed. This is also a culminating activity for the participants and is of use for the facilitator in knowing what they found most beneficial. See the handout.

    b. <u>Group Project</u>: If needed, work individually at home on assigned tasks within the project.

    c. <u>Emotions Log, Meditations, and Reflections</u>: Remind participants to complete these daily.

    d. <u>RAK</u>: Ask each participant to continue to do something good for a family member, people in the neighborhood, and the community (e.g., public spaces, the workplace, or school).

    e. <u>Wisdom</u>: This week's collected wisdom will be related to taking personal action to create positive change in a community.

SESSION SEVEN HANDOUTS

BUILDING A BETTER MAN LETTER

Thank you for participating in this group, which explores issues affecting young men in our society. We are very interested in your opinions and feedback.

For today, **please write a letter** to yourself or to a young man who will participate in the next Building a Better Man group. Think about **what you have learned here, what your goals are for the coming year, or what advice you can give to a person who will be participating in this group later**.

We may share your letter in a future Building a Better Man group, or in talks we give about these issues. The letters will be anonymous and no information will be given about you.

_____

_____

_____

_____

_____

_____

_____

_____

_____

_____

_____

_____

_____

_____

_____

_____

_____

_____

_____

_____

_____

_____

_____

SESSION EIGHT

Area of Focus: Community Involvement and Summary
Topic: Staying Connected and Getting "Better"
Goals:

- To summarize and consolidate learning from all previous sessions
- To learn how to continue using the skills gained in sessions

Discussion Questions for this Session:

1. What are you taking with you from the group?
2. What was most useful to you?
3. What do you need to do to continue to grow as a man?

Agenda:

I. Opening Act
   a. Introductions
   b. Group Creed
   c. Read the Building a Better Man Letters
   d. Sharing
   e. Prepare for the Group Project Presentation
II. Headliner
   a. Presentation of Group Project and Final Ceremony
III. After Party
   a. Review All Homework Activities

SESSION EIGHT BREAKDOWN

I. Opening Act

    a. Introductions (for boys and young men): Parents, caregivers, and family members are invited to this final session. Participants should introduce their guests.

    b. Group Creed.

    c. Read the Building a Better Man Letters: Not all participants may want to do this, but they are encouraged to volunteer. Another option is for the facilitator to read them anonymously.

    d. Sharing: Briefly discuss any of the usual homework activities.

    e. Prepare for the Group Project Presentation: Have the participants ready themselves and their guests for the presentation. Have audio/video equipment available if needed.

II. Headliner

    a. <u>Presentation of the Group Project and Final Ceremony</u>: This session should be a celebration of the hard work each participant put into the group, and it should have a true commencement feel to it. Emphasize the fact that this is only the initial step for each participant, and that much remains to be done by each. In advance of the session, prepare a review workbook for each participant to take home. This will help remind them of lessons learned and activities completed in group, and will promote generalization. Encourage participants to stay in contact and to support each other.

III. After Party

    a. Encourage participants to continue completing activities as part of their regular routine. Provide blank forms of all After Party homework so that they can make copies and continue using them. Discuss other ways to regularly engage in self-assessment, additional goal setting, etc.

    b. The facilitator should follow up with participants and/or parents for a brief exit interview within 2–3 days after the final session, and then make another contact at a set interval (e.g., three weeks) to assess status and progress.

6

BUILDING A BETTER MAN SYSTEMIC APPLICATION

The Building a Better Man group syllabus is a stand-alone intervention that is suitable for all age ranges and settings. Implemented independent of a larger framework, it will deliver all the key educational points that encourage *sustained* violence reduction and increased prosocial behavior while honoring the positive aspects of male socialization and self-improvement in an empirically driven manner. Hence, it can be incorporated into the overall psychoeducational and/or therapeutic programming of a variety of settings from YMCAs to adult detention facilities.

However, it can also form the core of a larger change program that provides a more powerful upstream and ecological *preventative* punch. Given the state of our American males, a primary care-type approach that features promotion of appropriate models of masculinity and prevention of violence and antisocial behavior will be most effective in the long run. Our emphasis on *protecting, educating, and connecting* males of all ages can be significantly furthered through the group syllabus when it resides within a larger framework.

Education about masculinity can take place in any situation regardless of how protected and connected males in the group are. It can be delivered in a "safe" place (e.g., a YMCA) where there is a modicum of control and security for group members while they are there. Unfortunately, the lessons learned and new skills developed by members in such a group can be diminished once they leave the confines of that safe place and return to their relatively uncontrolled and insecure environments. This has been a perennial problem for psychology—how to make new skills and behaviors learned in therapy generalize to real world settings. The Building a Better Man effort is not immune to this problem, which is why we need to consider a broader application that bolsters protection and connection within each group member's environment—from the intimacy of the home to the broader context of the community. Only then can we overcome the generalization problem, by simply making it moot. When the real world mimics the therapeutic setting as much as possible, new attitudes and behaviors will not need to generalize to something different.

Keeping in mind the focus on protecting, educating, and connecting our boys and young men, we consider as a template the Harlem Children's Zone (HCZ) approach. Aimed at breaking the cycle of generational poverty, Geoffrey

Canada's program in New York City holds promise because it seeks to change the community that surrounds a child *instead* of focusing on individual children.[1] This is a principle that is employed by other successful but relatively narrow social/educational change efforts such as the Strive project in Ohio[2] and the Comprehensive Support model,[3] both of which approach the problem of academic underachievement through collaboration with multiple centers of influence within a community. The two fundamental principles of the HCZ are to help children as early in their lives as possible and to create a critical mass of adults around them who can shepherd these youngsters into adulthood. What started as a city block-sized intervention has now expanded into an initiative with national import, endorsed by the Obama administration.

While the HCZ has generally been praised for its unique approach to curing the generational poverty of the Harlem community, because of its relative newness as an educational and social service organization, there is not a great deal of available data upon which to analyze it. Hence, there has been some hesitancy to replicate it in other cities.[4] What can be said, however, is that it certainly holds a lot of promise because of its ecological approach to the problem, seeking to address *all* the negative influences that have plagued that area of New York City—some of these quite entrenched (e.g., economic destitution, racism, and the breakdown of the nuclear family). It essentially attempts to change the equation, minimizing the weighting of those negatives and maximizing the positives, essentially shifting the culture *surrounding* individuals over time. In this regard, it mimics Bronfenbrenner's approach to behavior change, which has certainly been praised over the decades as having significant power to do that.[5] Preliminary data out of the HCZ school system does suggest that educational outcomes for its students are improved; as the Heritage Foundation's assessment states: "There seems little doubt that the HCZ is having a dramatic impact on the lives of those children and their families in their programs."[6]

A similar ecological approach can be used to address generational violence, encouraging nothing less than a cultural shift with regard to the continued propagation of narrowly defined conceptualizations of masculinity in our society that promote the violent resolution of conflict and the maxims: *be tough*, *be stoic*, *acquire things*, and *rely on no one*. The approach is relevant for any cohort of boys regardless of culture, color, religion, or socioeconomic status, as the prevalence of violence—to varying degrees—seems nearly universal in our society. The program combines a number of empirically based behavior change interventions that have been derived from the respective literature for each, focusing on the key elements of *protection, education, and connection*.

PROTECTION

When considering the protection and guidance of the young, the most important environment is the home. It is here where critical long-term social learning occurs. In his decades-long work on aggression in youth, Patterson proposed his seminal developmental model of aggressive behavior predicated on the notion that ineffective parental management practices and continuous coercive interactions between family members essentially train children and adolescents to act aggressively.[7] Many factors influence the development of coercion within a family, including demographics, parental traits, and current stress.[8] This is why it is important for a comprehensive intervention to address all of these as much as possible, particularly support for father/father figures (if they are indeed present). In cases where they are not present (admittedly, there are many) that support shifts to whoever is the primary caregiver, typically mother/mother figures (who become the de facto adult role model for their sons). There is certainly support in the literature for the appropriate involvement of fathers/ father figures for boys and young men, in that when this involvement is absent or abusive, the outcomes for these youngsters are significantly negatively affected.[9] This is also supported in research on post-divorce families that shows that elementary school-age boys have fewer behavior problems when they live with their fathers.[10]

With regard to media influences contributing to violence and antisocial behavior, these have been discussed in Chapter 2, but it is important to further describe them here when considering the protective element of a behavior change intervention. This is because of the pervasive nature of modern media and the nearly nonstop exposure that vulnerable boys and young men have to it. It has essentially become part of the microsystem layer in Bronfenbrenner's ecology, directly affecting males in their own homes. Children and adolescents all have learning vulnerabilities when it comes to exposure to violence. This is due to the still-developing brain, particularly the cerebral cortex, which will eventually give them the higher cognitive, emotional, sensory, and motor function they need to thrive in the world. Prior to this state of full development (not reached until the mid-twenties), their ability to handle disturbing/violent stimuli is obviously not the same as that of an adult because of these age-related mental limitations. The resultant vulnerabilities are many and include the premature assimilation and accommodation of harmful experiences leading to desensitization; overgeneralization and exaggeration of experiences that can create anxiety; and underdeveloped judgment that makes it difficult to put experiences into perspective. All of this can potentially lead to a developmental trauma (i.e., a gradual psychological harm resulting from exposure over time) akin to the immediate negative effects of a single but intense traumatic event. Anderson and Dill developed the General Affective Aggression model to describe this effect, positing that, through repeated exposure to violent media, a child with an already aggressive personality will be biased toward using aggression to interact with others or attempt to solve problems.[11]

With regard to violent content on television, literally thousands of studies conducted over the last 40 years point to one general conclusion: exposure to video media violence is clearly one factor contributing to the development of aggression.[12] There are identified short-term and long-term effects, the latter being most concerning as increased risk for violence over time can occur given a high and steady diet of violent content in television shows. Videogame influences have not been as thoroughly studied, given the relative newness of the medium. Findings to date have not been as conclusive, but they do at least suggest similar short-term effects.[13] While the debate continues about the influence of video games on behavior, there is certainly concern among many that the effects will be greater due to the interactive and repetitive learning aspects of the medium, the player's identification with a violent character, the realism of the violence, and the reinforcing nature of the activity. Regardless of the eventual outcome of future studies as to the power of the effect (or lack of it), when we consider variables that promote nonviolence and prosocial behavior, violent videogames would certainly not make that list.

Hence, key protective elements for boys and young men in the Building a Better Man systemic application include:

- sanctuaries where boys and young men can feel safety and trust in discussing the intimate details of their lives and in trying new ways of behaving (e.g., YMCA, Boys and Girls Clubs, afterschool programs);
- education to parents/caregivers about coercive family process and how to avoid it;

- guarantees from parents/caregivers that they will maintain a "clean" media environment in their homes, free of violent and pornographic content;
- alternative media that will satisfy the electronic needs of boys and young men;
- education of fathers or father figures focusing on generative fatherhood (learning and passing on fathering skills);
- ongoing support of fathers/father figures and their families (e.g., mentoring, employment/financial assistance, healthcare).

EDUCATION

An educational component is at the heart of an ecological intervention. It is the necessary and important act of helping boys and young men understand the variables that influence their behavior. Without this understanding, the motivation to change a way-of-being will be more difficult to obtain. As with any empirically based behavior change program, providing rationales, modeling new behavior, providing practice opportunities with feedback, and encouraging generalization to the real world are essential.[14] This formalized training process is interwoven throughout the Building a Better Man groups intervention described in the last chapter.

As described in Chapter 4, an effective violence prevention educative effort for males should:

- begin early in the lifespan;
- be sustained through incorporation into school curriculums or afterschool programs;
- become more sophisticated incrementally to match the cognitive and emotional development of participants;
- be engaging, interactive, and action oriented;
- be culturally sensitive;
- include intrapersonal, interpersonal, and community involvement oriented competencies;
- develop a menu of different skills and strategies to choose from in coping with life's challenges;
- encourage personal responsibility and a hard-work ethic;
- acknowledge the positive and negative consequences of changing behavior, providing support and resources to enhance sustained change.

In general, using a strength-based conceptual approach as outlined in the Positive Psychology/Positive Masculinity model is certainly indicated. As described in Chapter 3, this will help promote the well-being of boys and young men, giving them the tools to determine what aspects of masculinity are appropriate and what are not. Kiselica and Englar-Carlson contend that this approach has been shown to be successful in establishing and maintaining a strong working alliance with particularly hard-to-reach groups of boys and men. They further suggest that this will make it easier to motivate participants to change their behavior when it comes time to address their more problematic ways-of-being.[15]

Part and parcel of an educative effort are opportunities to try new skills and change behavior in a transformative way, not just through everyday experiences (e.g., intensive retreats and adventure therapy). Indeed, both the everyday and the "mountaintop" experiences are likely needed to sustain a new way-of-being because they complement each other.[16] For example, skills learned and practiced daily through interactive education can be put to the test in physically/mentally challenging, intensive, and time-limited situations. Seeing that new skills and behaviors work in these situations subsequently provides reinforcement to boys/young men and helps sustain behavior change in their less challenging everyday experiences.

Hence, key educative elements for boys and young men in the Building a Better Man systemic application include:

- recognition and expression of broader emotional needs;
- inclusion of nurturing as a paternal responsibility within families;
- acceptance of nonaggression-based definitions of masculinity;
- understanding of healthy sexuality;
- positive aspects of the provider/protector role;
- awareness of society's mixed messages about aggression/violence and overconsumption.

CONNECTION

Buss contends that males have an evolutionary bias toward discounting the future, meaning they live for the here-and-now, valuing immediate goods over future goods.[17] This orientation is likely the result of the dangerous roles men have generally assigned themselves in ancient and modern societies such as hunting, exploring, and soldiering. There exist a multitude of sayings that reflect this orientation, from the biblical "Eat, drink, and be merry for tomorrow we die" to the modern "Life sucks, then you die." Indeed, many young men, particularly in lower socioeconomic racial minority groups, firmly believe they will not live into their twenties. Sadly, crime and mortality statistics tend to bear this out.[18]

It is this short-term immediate orientation in males that restricts their participation in family life and in their communities. It nearly becomes a self-fulfilling prophecy in that males who insulate themselves from others tend to become less social, more egotistical, and hence view their communities and society with suspicion and react aggressively, putting themselves and others at risk for harm.

Hence, an important part of a program designed to decrease violence and increase prosocial behavior would be to instill in males a sense of community and cooperation, encouraging them to think more positively about their future and in the long term. It is a sense of enfranchisement, ownership, and belonging that can help push this behavior change in the desired direction. Simply put: when a young man feels valued by his community, he is more invested in it.

Unfortunately, in many communities men in general can set a negative tone because of their orientation and behavior. They can be feared by their families, friends, and neighbors. This in turn causes the community to also turn inward, becoming selfish and protective, until ultimately neighborhoods disintegrate.

Helping young men see how important they are to their communities becomes critical, because it is simply a fact that they *are important* whether in a negative or positive sense. Connecting them with their local social and spiritual organizations can help them to see that they are responsible, valued, and should invest in their futures. Rites of passage movements as espoused by Marx and others[19] are one way of establishing a sense of place, importance, and belonging for young men in their communities. Proponents of these guided and culturally appropriate experiences contend that this is what has been missing in modern society, whereas in more traditional or homogeneous societies the passage into manhood was clearly defined and, as a result, a young man felt connected and part of the adult community. The transformative experiences noted above could also become a means by which this acceptance into adulthood is felt by young men.

Garbarino's "monastery" example is another approach to the issue of disconnection, focusing on the deeper spiritual needs of boys and young men.[20] He cites examples of how spiritually grounded, nonpunitive religion can buffer adolescents against depression and help them resist a host of harmful behaviors. Care, mutual respect, and discipline are prominent features of this approach, which seeks to temporarily insulate and remove young men from the negative influences around them. This can be done physically through longer-term residential care, retreats, camps, or other residential programs of a temporary nature that seek to reestablish connection with others and their own inner selves, followed by regular practice opportunities in their home communities. This spiritual approach emphasizes the importance of contemplation, reflection, service, cooperation, meditation, and peace.

The spiritual aspect of young men's lives is not just defined by religion. Rather, it can be more broadly conceptualized as a sense of a higher power and of a future for the world and the soul. Organized nonpunitive western religion can play a significant role in this effort of course, but so can the other great religious traditions and the ancient disciplines and practices found in other cultures around the world (e.g., Native American philosophy, Far Eastern martial arts and meditative practices). All these efforts seek to diminish the influence of the here-and-now, foreshortened future orientation that is so common among young men, slowing things down and stretching time out.

Hence, key elements of connection for boys and young men in the Building a Better Man systemic application include:

- service to community organizations and schools;
- involvement in religious/spiritual activities;
- participation in team sports and the martial arts;
- participation in guided and culturally appropriate rites of passage experiences.

SUMMARY

A sustained presence in the community is essential to be a truly ecological and lifespan-oriented effort—for boys become young men who become older men, and the cycle continues with a new generation. Canada and his supporters clearly understand this as it relates to generational poverty. The effort must be comprehensive, involve multiple centers of influence, and be sustained in order to be effective in the long run. Generational conditions within a community dictate the way individuals who live there behave. Changing that behavior requires changing those preexisting conditions—and that simply takes time, probably measured generationally.

As the HCZ has shown, if a toe-hold can be established in a community, then through an ecological approach that continuously applies pressure over time more comprehensive change can occur and spread in that community. What Canada hopes for is that a tipping point will be reached in Harlem, one that will permanently change the culture there. We applaud his determination and adherence to a comprehensive, lifespan-oriented plan for the residents of his community. The approach is sound—it makes intuitive and scientific sense. As he has stated with regard to the educative aspect of HCZ:

If your mission is about all of the students in a community, then dealing with family crises, gangs, drugs, violence, and health all become part of your strategy to support development of the whole child, not just how they perform on standardized tests.[21]

His comment was in response to a preliminary analysis of educational outcomes within the HCZ completed in 2009, which, although favorable, did not review the multiple other components of the program that intertwine with education, simply because not enough data was available or fundamentally easy to assess.[22] However, in considering the approach of an ecological program such as the HCZ and how effective it might be, one is again reminded of Father Flanagan's motto: "There are no bad boys. There is only bad environment, bad training, bad example, and bad thinking." Perhaps there is a precedent of sorts for the HCZ in the Boys Town model.

Essentially, the Boys Town main campus in Omaha addresses all of those negatives through an incredibly consistent community system that is protective, educative, and connective in all respects. Indeed, the campus is an incorporated town with its own government, emergency services, school system, religious institution, and neighborhoods. All entities within the town operate on the same behavior modification system, with rewards and consequences established for its very diverse population to function within. All adults in this community— from family teachers in the family-home system, to school teachers, police, and priests—are there to protect, educate, and connect with. Anecdotally, the model's longevity, endowment, and popularity speak to its effectiveness. Long and short-term quantitative outcomes data generally supports this impression as well.[23]

There is of course some artificiality to be found in a setting like this. For example, the community does not suffer from economic deprivation or crime, there are no realistic negative influences (such as gangs or drugs), the adults are all carefully chosen and are employees of the organization, and even the population of residents is carefully chosen for their amenability to the model. Yet, Boys Town does provide a storied example of how behavior change (i.e., a decrease in violence and an increase in prosocial behavior) can occur given an ecological and sustained approach, where a community of adults make clear what their expectations, priorities, and hopes are for their young people.

The ultimate goal of an upstream or ecological approach to protecting, educating, and connecting boys and young men is to foster *sustained* violence reduction, while still honoring the positive aspects of male socialization. Given the above, it would be important for those of us committed to the study of males and masculinity to engage in political lobbying at local, state, national, and international levels so that an ecological approach itself can be sustained through grants, publicity, and endorsement by those in power. This appears to have been the case for Canada's HCZ and for iconic institutions like Boys Town. The Building a Better Man approach that specifically targets boys/young men and how they relate to their own masculinity can become a key part of that effort, for, in targeting that group, we also target the behaviors that arguably cause the most difficulty, heartache, and pain in our society.

Our lobbying effort and the subsequent fruit of that effort should focus on protecting boys, promoting their education in a balanced way, and connecting them with their communities. It should also focus on broader work–life changes for men so that they can participate more fully in their own families, power sharing and socioeconomic opportunity for minorities and women that decrease the growing gulf between rich and poor, sustainable consumption of natural resources, and a shift away from a national (in)security view of the world that promotes bellicosity.

Those of us who work for the betterment of society through mental health care, social work, medicine, and public policy are inherently optimistic. We must believe in momentum shifts and small but simultaneously numerous social changes that can lead to significant and dramatic societal improvements. In Malcolm Gladwell's bestselling book *The Tipping Point*, he states this quite succinctly:

> In the end, Tipping Points are a reaffirmation of the potential for change and the power of intelligent action. Look at the world around you. It may seem like an immovable, implacable place. It is not. With the slightest push—in just the right place—it can be tipped.[24]

NOTES

1. Harlem Children's Zone. The HCZ Project. Retrieved from: http://www.hcz.org/index.php/about-us/the-hcz-project.
2. Kania, J. & Kramer, M. (2011). Collective impact. *Stanford Social Innovation Review, 9(1), Winter 2011*.
3. Obiakor, F., Utley, C., Smith, R., & Harris-Obiakor, P. (2002). The comprehensive support model for culturally diverse exceptional learners: Intervention in an age of change. *Intervention in School and Clinic, 38(1)*, 14–27.
4. The Heritage Foundation (2013). Center for Policy Innovation, Discussion Paper #08 on Education (Hanson, D.). Assessing the Harlem Children's Zone.
5. Bronfenbrenner, U. (1979). Contexts of child rearing: Problems and prospects. *American Psychologist, 34*, 844–850.
   Bronfenbrenner, U. (1986). Ecology of the family as a context for human development: Research perspectives. *Developmental Psychology, 22*, 723–742.
   Bronfenbrenner, U. (1989, April). *The developing ecology of human development*. Paper presented at the Society for Research in Child Development meeting, Kansas City, MO.
6. The Heritage Foundation (2013). Assessing the Harlem Children's Zone, p. 8.
7. Patterson, G.R. (1982). *Coercive family process*. Eugene, OR: Castalia.
8. Patterson, G.R., Dishion, T.J., & Bank, L. (1984). Family interaction: A process model of deviancy training. *Aggressive Behavior, 10*, 253–267.
9. Garbarino, J. (1999). *Lost boys: Why our sons turn violent and how we can save them*. New York: The Free Press.
   Weintraub, K.J. & Gold, M. (1992). Monitoring and delinquency. *Criminal Behavior and Mental Health, 1(3)*, 268–281.
   Harper, C.C. & McLanahan, S.S. (2004). Father absence and youth incarceration. *Journal of Research on Adolescence, 14(3)*, 369–397.
10. Santrock, J. & Warshak, R. (1979). Father custody and social development in boys and girls. *Journal of Social Issues, 35(4)*, 112–125.
    Peterson, J. & Zill, N. (1986). Marital disruption, parent–child relationships, and behavior problems in children. *Journal of Marriage and the Family, 45*, 295–307.
    Camara, K. & Resnick, G. (1988). Interparental conflict and cooperation: Factors moderating children's post-divorce conflict. In E. Hetherington & J. Arasteh (Eds.). *Impact of divorce, single parenting, and stepparenting on children* (pp. 169–195). Hillsdale, NJ: Erlbaum.
    Maccoby, E., Depner, C., & Mnookin, R. (1988). Custody of children following divorce. In E. Hetherington & J. Arasteh (Eds.). *Impact of divorce,*

single parenting, and stepparenting on children (pp. 91–114). Hillsdale, NJ: Erlbaum.

11. Anderson, C.A. & Dill, K.E. (2000). Video games and aggressive thoughts, feelings, and behavior in the laboratory and in life. *Journal of Personality and Social Psychology, 78(4)*, 772–790.

12. Huesmann, L., Moise-Titus, J., Podolski, C., & Eron, L. (2003). Longitudinal relations between children's exposure to TV violence and their aggressive and violent behavior in young adulthood: 1977–1992. *Developmental Psychology, 39(2)*, 201–221.

13. Nicoll, J.M. & Kieffer, K.M. (2005). *Violence in video games: A review of the empirical literature.* Paper presented at the annual meeting of the American Psychological Association, Washington, DC, August 19, 2005.

14. Dowd, T. & Tierney, J. (1992). *Teaching social skills to youth.* Boys Town, NE: The Boys Town Press.

    Elliott, S.N. & Gresham, F.M. (1991). *Social skills intervention guide: Practical strategies for social skills training.* Circle Pines, MN: American Guidance Service.

15. Kiselica, M.S. & Englar-Carlson, M. (2010). Identifying, affirming, and building upon male strengths: The positive psychology/positive masculinity model of psychotherapy with boys and men. *Psychotherapy Theory, Research, Practice, Training, 47(3)*, 276–287.

16. Scheinfeld, D., Rochlen, A., & Buser, S. (2011). Adventure therapy: A supplementary group therapy approach for men. *Psychology of Men and Masculinity, 12(2)*, 188–194.

17. Buss, D.M. (2009). The great struggles of life: Darwin and the emergence of evolutionary psychology. *American Psychologist, 64(2)*, 140–148.

18. Federal Bureau of Investigation Uniform Crime Reports (2011). *Crime in the United States 2011.* Retrieved from: http://www.fbi.gov/about-us/cjis/ucr/ crime-in-the-u.s/2011/crime-in-the-u.s.-2011.

    Department of Justice, Bureau of Justice Statistics, National Crime Victimization Survey (2011). *Criminal victimization 2011.* Retrieved from: http://www.bjs.gov/content/pub/pdf/cv11.pdf.

    Department of Justice, Office of Juvenile Justice and Delinquency Prevention (2012). *Statistical briefing book.* Retrieved from: http://www.ojjdp. gov/ojstatbb/crime/jar.asp.

    Centers for Disease Control and Prevention, Division on Violence Prevention (2011). *Fatal injury reports, national and regional, 1999–2010.* Retrieved from: http://www.cdc.gov/violenceprevention/nvdrs/index.html.

19. Marx, F. Warrior Films—Rites of Passage. *Warrior Films—Rites of Passage* (Web). Retrieved from: http://www.warriorfilms.org/rites-of-passage/.

    Scheer, S.D., Gavazzi, S.M., & Blumenkrantz, D.G. (2007). Rites of passage during adolescence. *Forum for Family and Consumer Issues, 12(2).* Retrieved from: http://ncsu.edu/ffci/publications/2007/v12-n2-2007-summer-fall/scheer. php.

20. Garbarino, J. (1999). *Lost boys.*

21. The Heritage Foundation (2013). Center for Policy Innovation, Discussion Paper #08 on Education (Hanson, D.), p. 4.

22. Whitehurst, G. & Croft, M. (2010). *The Harlem Children's Zone, promise neighborhoods, and the broader, bolder approach to education.* The Brookings Institution, Brown Center on Education Policy at Brookings, July 20, 2010. Retrieved from: http://www.brookings.edu/research/reports/2010/07/20-hcz-whitehurst.

23. Boys Town National Research Institute for Child and Family Studies (2011). *2011 Applied Research Bibliography.* Retrieved from: http://lb2.boystown.org/

sites/default/files/2011%20Bibliography%20-%20External%20Website%20Version%20%284.4.12%29.pdf.

24. Gladwell, M. (2002). *The tipping point: How little things can make a big difference* (p. 259). New York: Back Bay Books.

CHAPTER **7**

TEN THINGS
YOU CAN DO

In July of 2010, Lebron James held the sporting world captive as he announced his long-anticipated decision regarding where he would take his basketball talents for the next few seasons of his professional career. When he selected the Miami Heat, he immediately put a lot of pressure on himself by stating he did not come to win a championship, but *multiple* championships. At the end of his first year in Miami, his team lost in the NBA Finals. The media mocked him; but instead of feeling sorry for himself, he dedicated his efforts over the next summer to taking his game to an even higher level. The next year, the Heat did win the NBA Championship. But instead of being content with this achievement, he worked harder again during the off season, in part because he understood that if his vision of multiple championships was to materialize, he would need to continue to work twice as hard to *remain* a champion. Mr. James understood the nature of his personal challenge and then worked hard to obtain it. He understood what it would take to reach the summit, *and* what it would take to stay there.

Once a goal is attained, we cannot rely solely on past achievements to keep us where we want to be. If we do, we will soon be reminiscing about the good old days, instead of moving forward. When we come to the realization that change is necessary to improve our lives, we must also understand that this is not an easy process. To matriculate through a journey of self-discovery and rebuilding, we must be able to identify significant problems in our lives, identify solutions to those problems, implement those solutions, and then evaluate their success. Nelson Mandela stated it thus: "it always seems impossible, until it is done."

This concluding chapter will highlight ten ideas and activities that a man can use to help move himself higher up the Masculinity Developmental Hierarchy pyramid. These are practical, strength-based, and action-oriented personal objectives that can be used in daily life to promote continual growth and avoid/reduce antisocial or even violent behavior. Some of these are philosophical and motivational in nature; others are aligned more closely with the group sessions in Chapter 5.

The chapter concludes with a similar list for parents/caregivers of boys and young men, providing the same practical, strength-based, and action-oriented ideas and activities to help them continue to move forward in their lives and in their development as mentally, emotionally, and physically healthy males who have a solid understanding of their own manhood.

TEN THINGS YOU CAN DO TO HELP YOURSELF

Within the Masculinity Developmental Hierarchy, your initial learning and training takes place in the Dependent Acquisition stage. When that initial instruction has either encouraged a narrowly defined view of masculinity or been compromised and corrupted by various negative internal and external influences, it is likely that you will be limited in your view of gender roles and in your subsequent actions. This *can* lead to a lack of interpersonal awareness, dysfunction in relationships with others, and withdrawal from or negative involvement in your communities. Recognizing that these *are* limitations is key to your own cognitive retraining and personal behavior modification.

If you suspect that you are in need of change in this way, consider these ten ideas and activities that may help to improve your standing and maximize your potential:

1. Self-Inventory
2. Stack Success
3. Positive Associations
4. Daily Evaluations
5. Healthy Living
6. Financial Literacy
7. Companions
8. Emotional Colonoscopy
9. Helping Others
10. Continue to Grow.

#1 Self-Inventory

Self-knowledge is essential to healing and growth. This will require you to pause, slow down, and accurately self-assess. Every successful business starts with a successful plan. The SWOT analysis from Session Three in the group syllabus (Chapter 5)—adapted from the business world—can be that successful personal start for you. In his national best seller *The 7 Habits of Highly Effective People*, Steven Covey states that a person must begin with the end in mind, like a great architect.[1] In order to increase the chances of achieving that successful end, you need to take inventory and determine what you have and what you need. What are your plan's strengths and resources; what are its weaknesses? What are your opportunities and what are threats that can derail the "business of you"? See Session Three for more details and the SWOT analysis matrix. The matrix can be used to provide a framework for short and long-term goals.

#2 Stack Success

Mike McCarthy, Head Coach of the Green Bay Packers, understands how the attainment of small goals can lead to an ultimate goal. When talking to his players, he conveys the importance of looking at each game individually, and then breaking down a long 16-game season into four quarters. At the end of each quarter (four games) the team assesses their weaknesses and flaws. But, even more importantly, he tries to build into his players a mindset of winning. He talks about "stacking success." Each victory propels the team to win another game and another game. He understands that, with each victory, the attitude and confidence for future success increase. Winning is contagious. And this is something you want to contract and spread.

Consider the example of a new boxing prospect who many believe has what it takes to be a champion. The trainers and managers initially schedule four-round fights with weaker opponents that the prospect should easily beat. With each victory, the prospect learns more and gains more confidence. Next, they schedule a fight against either another young prospect on the rise or a seasoned veteran a bit past his prime. After successes against these worthy opponents, the challenge of serious contenders and the reigning champion await. The prospect, who has risen from contender to legitimate challenger, is filled with confidence from his training and successful past. When the prospect does win the championship, he is not surprised. He simply believes he has accomplished his goal—obtained his rightful destiny. As it is in the world of sports, this also pertains to success for you. The question becomes: "How do you stack success?"

Do this by establishing an attainable goal for yourself. The key is to simply start moving forward. For example, if your goal is to do 100 sit-ups, just do one the first day. It seems simple, but *that* is the key. Reward yourself for trying. One seems ridiculously easy of course, but consider how many days you have done zero. The next day continue to stack success by doing two sit-ups. And so on until you have reached your goal. If you want to read a book, you can spread that out over 200 days, and increase the number of pages read by one each successive day. The goal is to start and create a timeline to help you stay on track. See Session Four in the group syllabus for more detail and a goal-setting handout. The goal is important, but you must properly manage your progress to make it a reality. The focus is to start with smaller objectives, complete them, and use these "emotional trophies" as a catalyst.

#3 Positive Associations

The famous motivational speaker Jim Rohn stated that "you are the average of the five people you spend the most time with." When we consider people, we think of them as the four most basic mathematical symbols. We see each person as an addition, subtraction, multiplication, or division. We think of ourselves as an investment of one million dollars. Our goal is to successfully invest that we might see a profit. As a result, we will associate with multiplication and addition more often than subtraction and division. When we consider multiplication, we see people who can grow "the business of me" exponentially. These are people with solid words of wisdom, people who have power to change your conditions immediately for the better. When we look at *addition*, we see people who can grow us in a limited fashion, but not exponentially. These are people who add to your life in a positive fashion by their words and deeds. They help in a small but meaningful fashion.

When we consider *subtraction*, we see people who are well meaning, but are a bit too needy and usually not generous. Their needs are not unrealistic; they might be people who you don't mind helping. However, they do take more away from your value than what they give you. They need to borrow some money today or they need to tell you their problems, or they need a ride to the airport, and their needs seem to never end. The way to identify them is that "they need," consistently.

The subtraction, although needy, should be clearly distinguished from the *division*. This person will take your million dollars and leave you with one hundred. They divide your wealth. They are people who could destroy your works and world. This should not be confused with the notion of "helping yourself before helping others," or an individualistic need to put yourself first; but it is a call for you to choose your friends wisely and maintain balance in your interpersonal relationships. To help others is essential, and to think of the well-being of our families and community is part of our own well-being. However, at times those around us take too much from us, and we must be wise in our investment.

However, not all of the people who present as *division* are enemies. Just as in mathematics, multiplication and division are seen as very similar due to their reciprocal relationship. Some friends have ideas that are filled with great possibilities, but have low percentages for success. When we go along with their once in a lifetime opportunity, we often pay for their failures. There is a scene in a movie entitled *Jason's Lyric*[2] in which the female character pleads to her boyfriend to leave the city where they live. The boyfriend responds that he cannot leave because of his wayward brother. She then tells him that *she* has to leave because he's going to break her heart given that he keeps trying to save a man that doesn't want to be saved. Often times, we are confused with multiplication and division because we are blinded by love and family connections.

We encourage you to complete a Vision Board analysis (see Session Four in Chapter 5) on the people closest in your lives and see what they are to you on a most consistent basis. Place them in a category, but understand that situations can move people from an addition to a subtraction, even to a division. For example, certain conditions, such as alcohol consumption, may change a person's status. The key is to understand your friends on multiple levels and learn that your choice of friends impacts your life in multiple ways.

#4 Daily Evaluations

Every day presents different challenges. There is an axiom that states that "he who fails to plan, plans to fail." Wayne Dyer, the famous self-help author, will refer to the "Law of Intention" in a lot of his speeches and writings.[3] He champions the idea that we will attract what we are. What does this mean? In writings from antiquity, many philosophers will refer to the body as a vessel, with the bigger question being what is inside the vessel. Some days are better than other days, why? Most will say based on the situation, but we submit that it is the attitude of the individual. If the vessel is filled with compassion, knowledge, understanding, and love, there is not a situation that one cannot navigate through, regardless of the size of the storm. If our body is our vessel, we have to understand that we are leaking vessels and each day presents an opportunity for optimism and positivity to fill us—or for us to be consumed with bitterness, darkness, and pessimism.

The key to having a good day begins with having a good night. It is here that the Morning Meditations and Nightly Reflections are important (see Session Two in Chapter 5). Every night should be an opportunity for you to reflect on the past day. What went right? What went wrong? What is under my control to repair? At the end of the day, you have to be accountable and accept responsibility for your actions—forgiving and praising yourself as appropriate. In the morning, take a moment to pause and ready yourself for the day. This is accomplished by thinking with *intention*, to set the course for the day. What are your goals as they relate to you, family, work, and community? This time is essential, as you begin to fill that vessel for the day. It is imperative that you begin on a positive note with the intention to be good and think good. Pray, meditate, or ponder your "emotional chi."

For example, when our mornings begin with an unwelcomed alarm, thoughts of pressure for the day, coupled with unwelcomed chaos from loved ones and others, we pour sourness into our own vessels and that course will be set for the rest of the day. Of course, it would be irresponsible and incorrect to assert that a bad start will *automatically* ruin the whole day. However, let us look to a sprinter who runs a short race and ask him how important the start is to that race. If we are off to a bad start, then we must work double time to pour more positivity into our vessels through reframing our cognitions. Seek sources of motivation, inspiration, past triumphs, and even comic relief to help yourself do this. In short, you have to identify and use what helps to elevate you in difficult times, while avoiding those things that are counterproductive (e.g., illicit drug use).

#5 Healthy Living

Many people look for quick fixes in our society, others don't have that many options to begin with. However, if it took years for a problem to develop, you have to understand you cannot solve it in a few short days, weeks, or even months. Yet, people still seek immediate relief and want a solution that will help to ease some of the pain. Consider these four steps that will *begin* to put you on the path to recovery:

1. positive attitude
2. regular check-ups
3. proper exercise
4. adequate sleep.

Humans are creatures of habit. It is difficult for us to accept change, and it is even harder for us to willingly initiate it.[4] If you want something different, you must be willing to *try* something different. Psychotherapists have specific theoretical orientations they employ to help facilitate this. For example, those who subscribe to a cognitive-behavioral model believe that if you can alter thinking, the appropriate behavior will follow. Essentially, this is the power of positive thinking—or attitude—in action. This type of thinking skill is something that can be taught to you and then used as part of your daily routine.

The next two steps are perhaps the most difficult to sustain because they involve action rather than thought change. Before you embark on an exercise program or significant change in diet, it is imperative that you seek proper medical advice from a professional.[5] This requires a trip to your physician's office. Many in our country are without health insurance and will use this as an excuse as to why they do not seek medical attention for routine health concerns. The Affordable Care Act will ultimately help more Americans to have some form of insurance and access to routine care.[6] Still, men are less likely to seek the advice of a medical professional, and it is no secret that they have a shorter life span than women in America.[7] There are erroneous masculinity issues wrapped around this—such as the need to be perceived as tough and self-reliant. But if only a yearly physical is completed to check for blood sugars, cholesterol, and blood pressure levels, these basic checks can reveal much about overall health and can signal early warnings about issues that deteriorate over time, when left unchecked. Preventative maintenance is key to optimal health. At these visits, your goal is also to find an exercise program and balanced diet that promote a healthy lifestyle custom-made for your specific body.

Many Americans suffer from chronic fatigue, mainly caused by our sedentary lifestyles, poor diets, stress, and lack of adequate sleep. With regard to sleep for adults, it is commonly understood that somewhere between six and ten hours of *uninterrupted* rest is needed.[8] These hours should not be several naps logged together, but a sustained period of rest that allows the body to reach the fifth stage of sleep known as REM (Rapid Eye Movement).[9] As an exercise, log the hours of sleep you get each night and note what your energy level was like the next day. You will likely see a dramatic difference if you strive to get more rest.

#6 Financial Literacy

Money is a necessity in the world in which we live. Ironically, money management is not a part of the regular curriculum in most of our public schools. Financial fitness is just as important as physical fitness. Many people recognize that they need a physician or trainer to shape and sculpt their bodies. It is the same for their finances—a coach is needed. Many Americans have welcomed trainers like Richard Simmons, Billy Blanks, Jillian Michaels, Shaun T., and Tony Horton into their homes to help them transform their bodies. Financial health can be accomplished in the same way through the seminal financial writings of such experts as Clason,[10] Kiysaki,[11] Stanley and Danko,[12] Orman,[13] Hill,[14] and Harper.[15] They will all tell you that there are no real secrets, but only principles that require discipline and patience. Clason's classic *The Richest Man in Babylon* provides simple stories and easy to use steps. The gist of the money principles revolve around these steps. First, obtain a skill that can provide a steady stream of income. Second, develop this stream. Third, learn to spend conservatively. Fourth, learn to save. Fifth, look for solid opportunities to invest your savings. The goal is to avoid the conspicuous consumption mentality,[16] and keep saving and properly investing. And finally, learn how to give back time, talent, and treasure to help others.

#7 Companions

No man is an island unto himself. For you to be successful, you need seven companions in your life. These companions can help add positive value and move you toward that final stage of Active Awareness in the Maculinity Developmental Hierarchy pyramid.

1. *The Curator:* The curator is the elder statesman in your life, who is the guide that teaches you about history, the history of yourself, family, culture, and the world. Knowledge is power and this person is a wealth of valuable information. There is an African proverb that states that "when an old man dies, a library burns to the ground." We must find our own library to help us along our way, or else we will pay for the lessons we could have gotten for free.

2. *The Counselor:* Although there continues to be stigma associated with mental health, it is essential that we work to balance this with our physical health. Consider working from a paradigm of mental *wellness* instead of mental *illness*. The Affordable Care Act requires equity for mental health when compared to physical health coverage. And society as a whole has begun to recognize the importance of mental wellness, specifically because we all have family and friends who have been diagnosed with mental health conditions. It is important for you to have a counselor for three reasons. First, this is a professional who can guide you and/or connect you with people who can

help with mental wellness. Second, this counselor is a person with professional ethics and confidentiality, who will not talk about you to others. Lastly, it provides a setting in which your problems can be the true focus. When you talk to a "friend counselor," it is likely that you will have to hear *their* story as well. One will oblige a friend, even though they may not have enough emotional currency to attend to such a conversation. With professional counseling, your time is devoted solely to you.

3. *The Curtain:* The curtain is the one who "closes" for you. When a play is over, the curtain closes to let the crowd know it. The person in your life, in this role, is the one who helps you close the show. For example, for people pleasers, this is the person who will help you say "no," or say it for you. This is the person who will not let you get into a bad business deal. This is the person who will take the keys from you and not let you drive drunk. This is the person who is a pseudo bodyguard, protecting you, even from yourself.

4. *The Conscience:* This is the person who helps you set—and re-set—your moral compass. This companion is different from the Curtain, because he/she is more hands-off with their intervention. This is the friend who sits with you and listens to you, as a counselor, but has more of an intimate relationship with you. They do not judge you, but they are not afraid to call you out. This person will be there to help answer questions and research things for you.

5. *The Crazy One:* This is the friend that makes you have fun. This is the person that forces you to ask that girl out, go on that trip, to take the leap and start your own business, to let your child have that toy, to sign up for that triathlon, to allow you to not get stuck in a boring routine that stunts your growth and happiness. This is the friend you live through vicariously and who allows you to enter their world, where the entrance and exit ramps are in safe zones that do not violate your personal ethics and values.

6. *The Cousin:* This is one of your best friends, who can fulfill any of the roles above. This is your "Swiss Army Knife" buddy—at any given time he/she can provide for you the help you need. The cousin is the friend you can depend on for any and everything. This is a person who can make you laugh, hit you in the arm, loan you some money, uplift your spirits, even give you a kidney, and have your back without question.

7. *The Cradle:* This friend is the one who needs *you* more than you need him/her. It is important that you have someone who looks up to you and keeps you accountable. Having a person like this in your life works to your advantage in multiple ways. First, it allows you to provide support to others. This increases your self-esteem. Second, it provides a valuable service to your community. For example, teaching the next generation of men about such things as positive masculinity (see Session One in Chapter 5) ensures that solid principles are being passed on to those who are in that Dependent Acquisition stage, equipping them to deal with issues that lie ahead. Lastly, it is important to stay around young people to stay young yourself. Ironically, they will teach you a fair amount in return. Their often naïve and idealistic approach will help keep you inspired and hopeful.

#8 Emotional Colonoscopy

Most medical professionals agree the average age for men to begin preliminary testing for colon cancer is around 50.[17] This age may vary based on family history, but the key is to complete an early screen. The results will provide a detailed look into the large intestine and colon to find tumors, polyps, and ulcers. Before this procedure, you must clean out your system completely so that the entire gastrointestinal tract can be clearly seen. Failure to do this will prevent the procedure from yielding accurate results and it will have to be rescheduled. In Elijah Muhammad's book *How to Eat to Live*, he details the importance of the spiritual ritual of fasting as a necessary component in maintaining proper nutritional balance.[18] Even more so today, with our processed foods being deficient and sometimes toxic, it is necessary for us to have a short-term cleanse to help our body release toxins.[19]

These examples of physical cleanings are used to illustrate the need for a regular *mental* cleanse. As stated earlier, we are all vessels. We are trying to keep a clean vessel full of accurate and positive thoughts that increase our chances of having a positive daily experience of life. Weight loss experts like Dr. Ian Smith explain to their audiences that before a new diet can start, it is essential to remove the remaining waste of the previous faulty diet.[20] To start the new diet with remains of the old inside is tantamount to pouring new coffee into a dirty cup. As it is for the body, so it is for the mind.

Do a regular mental fast, similar to the one Elijah Muhammad recommends for the body, and then from time to time do a full-out emotional cleanse similar to preparing for a colonoscopy. There is an axiom that states "garbage in, garbage out." Your goal here is to abstain from what we allow into our vessels on a daily basis—to fast. Do this by relaxing in silence outside of the noise of television, radio, and idle chatter. Take time alone to pray, meditate, and clear out the emotional baggage that you may carry on a daily basis. Far too many times, we allow old wounds and hurts to sabotage and destroy the possibility of a better future. In a sense, we have become *emotional hoarders*—afraid to confront or just too busy to remove this emotional mess; sadly, this prevents us from going further. It prevents us from maximizing new things that are poured into our vessels. It is essential that you reserve time to cleanse your mind. It is during this emotional colonoscopy that you heal the wounds and keep your vessel clear of unwanted and toxic decay.

#9 Helping Others

Helping others allows us to heal ourselves. There are many people to help and many ways to help. There are many organizations and schools that appreciate and welcome volunteers. You will feel good when you give someone proper directions when they are lost, lead a little league team to a championship, help build a community playground, read to an elementary classroom, buy someone a gift for no special reason, or give someone a needed word of encouragement at the proper time. There is no deed too small. The goal is to deliver multiple random acts of kindness each day. Ask family members how you can help them or actively seek helping opportunities in your community. The goal is to go out every day with the expressed intent to help make life a little better for someone else.

#10 Continue to Grow

Put the responsibility on yourself to create a personalized list of what you need to continue to grow. General lists like the one described here are good and helpful, but no one will understand *you* like yourself. Maintain your growth by continuing to find things that meet your needs and that allow you to incorporate new ideas and wisdom. Remember the library idea above—visit it often. Another old axiom states: "Feed a man fish and you feed him for a day. Teach him how to fish and you feed him for a lifetime." No book or person can give you all the answers, but these can be catalysts that promote brainstorming your life. Continue the first nine steps above and you will learn how this tenth—and most important—step will come more effortlessly and in a shorter period of time.

TEN THINGS YOU CAN DO TO HELP YOUR SON

Generation X's and Y's were groomed for adulthood in an environment of immediate gratification. Therefore, it is important that the things we do as parents/caregivers to help them are filled with wisdom and are solidly informative, but also have a brisk pace and an element of multimedia entertainment. These ten steps are similar to the steps for men but are customized to be more age appropriate. In keeping with the axiom "it's hard to teach an old dog new tricks," the goal is to help our sons as they navigate through the Dependent Acquisition stage, creating a cocoon of positive influences around them. Consider these ten ideas and activities that may help improve your son's conception of his own masculinity and that maximize his potential:

1. Shower with Love
2. Social Learning
3. Rules
4. Home–School Collaboration
5. Activities
6. Three "F's"
7. Companions
8. Responsibilities
9. Helping Others
10. Continue to Grow.

#1 Shower with Love

In a homophobic society, many fathers are reluctant to express their love for their sons, fearing it may make them "gay" or "too soft." It is such thinking that teaches many boys to either hide their emotions or seek out other males—potentially of dubious distinction—for that connection.[21] This masculine suppression of a full range of appropriate emotions leaves our young men emotionally stunted and potentially hyper-aggressive, as noted previously in this book. The situation is exacerbated when a young man is missing parental figures in his life. It is imperative that we understand how important the first five years of a child's life are with regard to the ability to properly attach to a parent/caregiver. Child trauma specialist Bruce Perry, MD, states that attachment is the first of six core strengths that help to promote healthy emotional development.[22] When the attachment is strong, a child who is confident and independent is likely to emerge. Therefore, it is important to supply those basic needs of food, protection, and shelter; however, it is just as important to supply affection, comfort, and love *in abundance*. In the worst cases, severe and sustained abuse/neglect decreases the likelihood of positive attachments for children.

Relationship expert Dr. Gary Chapman states that love can be expressed in many ways by couples, and accordingly children.[23] This is important because sometimes there can be a disconnect between the parent and child and how affection is expressed and needed. Doctor Chapman goes on to say that children can be shown love in many different ways through words, touch, spending quality time, providing gifts, and services rendered. Often times, parents may believe that they get along with all their children *but* one. They will say they treat all of them exactly the same, but this "one" does not appreciate the love like the others. As parents, you are the ultimate coach; you must be willing to adapt to your players. The focus of this first point is to shower your son with love often, but in the way in which he needs it.

#2 Social Learning

In social psychology, we understand that children can be taught verbally, but the most effective form of instruction will be the behavior that is modeled right in front of them, with the most weight given to the most important persons in their lives—the parents/caregivers. We cannot tell our children one thing and then model another. Doctor Tony Roach, a psychospiritual motivator, states: "Children are wonderful observers, but poor interpreters." This is something every parent must understand. The knee-high private eye is in the room and sees all; however, the child may not be able to understand why certain behaviors are appropriate at one age, but not at another.[24] The key is to model the appropriate behavior you want to see from your son. Otherwise, he will model the inappropriate behavior.

All parents/caregivers have had the eerie experience that they handled a situation exactly as their parents did—and they kick themselves for it. The question is: What are you modeling to your son that he will repeat *now*? Parents and caregivers, ask yourself:

- Does my son see me (or people in my house) involved in alcohol and drug abuse?
- Does my son see me act out in physically and verbally aggressive ways?
- Has my son seen me go to the doctor for a basic check-up?
- Has my son seen me read a book?
- Does my son see me exercise?
- Does my son see me hug his mother?
- Does my son see me involved in sexually inappropriate activity?

#3 Rules

The Dalai Lama has said, "The more rules you create, the more rule breakers you make." Boys need rules, but they do not need an overabundance of them. It is best to follow these three guidelines:

1. *Be Fair:* The rules should be fair and appropriate. Do not set rules that will likely be too difficult for your son to follow. This is not a license to allow him to act inappropriately, but it is appropriate that he understand there will be rules and consequences if those rules are not followed. As a boy gets older, it is a good idea to give him some ownership in helping to set household rules.

2. *Be Firm:* It is important for a boy to understand that rules are *the rules*. He must understand that, like a referee in a sporting event, you will blow the whistle in an objective manner when a penalty has occurred. The key is not to be a dictator or tyrant in your rule, but to govern through an authoritative style that promotes discipline and a level of respect.

3. *Be Consistent:* This is the key guideline, as inconsistency will be the downfall of any discipline program. Parents who judge an infraction in a firm way

(i.e., black or white) but who later judge the same situation on a continuum (i.e., shades of gray), with a different consequence imposed than originally agreed upon, will find their son in a state of continual limit testing. Most players in an athletic event understand that each referee will officiate the game differently, but they also expect that he/she will be consistent over the course of the game and with both teams. Children are the same way. Lack of consistency leads to confusion and limit testing. Inconsistent discipline in the home can lead to rule-breaking outside it as well.

#4 Home–School Collaboration

In his book *Savage Inequalities*, Jonathon Kozol discussed the profound differences between urban and rural school communities when compared to their suburban counterparts. The assertion is not that the teachers did not care, but, like Chapman's love languages, they had a hard time connecting with students from different demographics than their own.[25] When a student and teacher do not academically connect, the student generally suffers the most. In a lot of these cases, according to education researcher Dr. Festus Obiakor, children that are culturally and linguistically different are often misunderstood, *mis*-assessed, *mis*-categorized, *mis*-placed in stigmatizing special education programs that have proven to be ineffective.[26] It would behoove you as parent/caregiver to investigate the teacher, the administrators, and the climate of the school before allowing your son to enroll. In cases where your options are limited, you must become active on the PTA, establish a cooperative relationship with the school, and work with your son on issues and potential issues immediately. This may not be easy to do. However, the goal is to—as much as possible—create a spirit of cooperation between you and school staff. In general, the most important thing a parent/caregiver can instill in a son is the absolutely critical importance of a proper education, including responsibility for his own behavior and overall school citizenship.

#5 Activities

Extra-curricular activities are important for boys and young men. They provide them with outlets to broaden their daily experiences, bring them into contact with other peers and adult role models, and play to strengths and talents that may not be evident in the school setting. Extra-curricular activities do not have to be limited to athletics. Here are ten examples and the potential benefits for your son:

1. *Contact Sports:* Sports such as boxing, football, martial arts, and hockey are appropriate outlets to release frustration and energy, while simultaneously tiring your son out. Contact sports essentially involve controlled aggression. When your son learns to stop at the whistle or the bell or the command of his sensei, he learns he can control his actions and emotions through discipline and the presence of a strong coach/guide.

2. *Team Sports:* Many parents are concerned about the growing literature on brain trauma (i.e., concussions) and the long-term effects of these injuries.[27] A good alternative for parents are other types of team sports (e.g., cross country, swimming) that reduce the likelihood of contact. Team sports (contact or noncontact) teach your son the importance of team work and accountability to others and help build those soft skills that will prove essential as he builds interpersonal relationships. They will also help your

son deal with the normal ebb and flow of life as his team handles the roller coaster of triumphant wins and heartbreaking losses.

3. *Individual Sports:* Team sports will help your son to develop social skills, but individual sports will help him develop his individual character. If a team loses, one can use others as an excuse, but in an individual sport (e.g., bowling, golf, archery) your son will learn that real competition is always within yourself. It is not about beating another person *per se* but about continual self-improvement. Individual sports are a fantastic way to increase self-esteem and teach children the benefits and importance of practice and study.

4. *Culinary Arts:* The purpose of an activity such as this is twofold: to help teach a valuable life skill and an activity that is outside the norm for most males. It will allow your son to be in an environment where control, discipline, and patience are essential. It will also help your son shape his conceptualization of gender roles.

5. *Art:* This includes drawing, painting, sculpting, and photography. These are excellent ways for your son to express himself and his deeper-seated emotions without having to talk that much about it.

6. *Musical Instruments*: Amy Chua's book *Battle Hymn of the Tiger Mother* describes one loving mother's belief in the importance of musical instruments.[28] Although some have questioned, even criticized, her mandate of daily two hour practices for her daughter, the importance of music and learning an instrument in the life of a child cannot be underestimated in terms of discipline and self-confidence. Mastering an instrument also translates into cognitive improvement in the core academic areas of mathematics and reading.

7. *Summer Educational Enrichment Camps:* What am I good at? What am I going to do when I grow up? Boys and young men can be confused about scholastic and vocational goals because their natural interests and aptitudes may not be tapped in the school setting. Summer programs offer classes in subject matter like engineering, carpentry, writing/journalism, architecture, politics, arts/theatre, and the sciences. Your goal as a parent/caregiver is to help your son reach a vocational epiphany, a life experience that immediately grabs them, hopefully matching them to something that resonates within their spirit.

8. *Boy Scouts:* This is a traditional organization that teaches boys and young men to be resourceful, self-reliant, group and community-oriented, and moral. Scouting is action-oriented and will get your son outside, teaching him to appreciate the natural world in the process.

9. *Something Outside of Their Comfort Zone:* The goal here is to stretch your son. Put him in an environment that will help force him to grow outside his own perceived limits and experience peers who do not look like him. This will help him develop a better understanding of others he is not normally accustomed to interacting with.

10. *Your Hobby:* As parents, we often participate in activities *for* our children, purely for their sake. We will endure activities and events we have absolutely no interest in. Perhaps without being overly aggressive about it, gently guide your son into an activity that you enjoy and are skilled at. If your son grows to love what you love, then it will provide a good outlet for you to positively communicate and interact.

#6 Three "F's"

Similar to your own improvement in the areas of healthy living and financial fitness noted above, consider these for your son:

- *Food:* The standard American diet is full of processed food, meat filled with steroids and antibiotics, monosodium glutamate (MSG), and high fructose corn syrup.[29] Even our fruits and vegetables have been grown in deficient soil while being simultaneously coated with all types of pesticides.[30] It's no surprise that our children are overstimulated, overweight, and suffering from multiple physical health disorders. There is an old adage that states "children are like puppies, they will eat what you give them." It is imperative that you provide your son with proper nutrition and avoid those foods that create and exacerbate poor health. It is also incumbent upon school systems and the government to help in geographic areas that have been labeled as "food deserts" and "food swamps" because of the lack of available nutritious food (e.g., inner cities).[31] It is essential that our medical professionals help children and families understand the benefit of fruits and vegetables. The goal is not to make every family vegan, but to simply understand the positive effects of an unprocessed or raw diet with super foods.[32]

- *Fitness:* It has become tradition that every First Lady champion a social cause that affects our nation. Nancy Reagan was known for her campaign against drug use by young people ("Just Say No"), and Laura Bush was recognized for her work on women's health. The current First Lady, Michelle Obama, has championed the cause of keeping our children fit with her "Let's Move" campaign. She understands that our children need to be fit and that they simply need to move their bodies more (at least 60 minutes a day).[33] These minutes can be accumulated in a variety of ways and at various times of the day, and frankly are excellent ways to address a boy's need to burn off energy. In conjunction with physical movement, parents/caregivers should use this as a time to "move" their sons (and daughters) to the office of various healthcare professionals (e.g., primary doctor, optometrists, dentists) for preventative checkups. These visits will normalize interactions with health-care providers from an early age and proactively foster a positive relationship with an industry that has been frankly avoided and ignored by some segments of our population.[34]

- *Financial Literacy:* Undisciplined children with money learn to be undisciplined adults with money. In a society built on consumerism, we must teach our sons to be good stewards of their resources. This includes knowing that money does not equate to happiness and does not solve all of your problems (and in fact it may create some), saving is more important than spending, money needs to be safeguarded, and money can be used to help others.

#7 Companions

One of the biggest social fallacies is that a woman cannot raise a boy to be a man. This is simply untrue. There are certainly lessons that can be more readily understood and transferred by a father to his son, but a mother can teach a male child to be a responsible and respectful person. A woman can teach a boy how to navigate romantic interpersonal relationships. In fact, she may be a better source than a man on matters that pertain to the opposite sex. And a father alone cannot teach a boy everything he needs to become a man. Every man has flaws, and if he is the sole teacher, the boy will likely inherit the same flaws. For a boy to become a well-rounded man, he needs instruction from multiple men and women. Here are the several companions that your son may benefit from, in addition to his parent/caregiver:

1. *The Coach:* This is the person (male or female) who serves as a parent figure for your son. They may be his music teacher, baseball coach, or youth minister. This person's role is to help validate the words of his parents. This person also helps to provide nurturing and a sense of belonging from someone who is not related to him.

2. *The Curator:* This is the grandparent figure who teaches lessons from the old school—those valuable life lessons that cannot be taught in a book, but only imparted through shared experiences and didactic conversations between elder and youngster. Boys benefit from that person who makes him feel special and who he can go to with questions about life.

3. *The Companion:* This is the best friend, equivalent to the "Cousin" for adults above. Every boy benefits from a best friend, someone who has his back. Whenever we see sitcoms featuring boys, there is always a friend for the main character. For every Wally, there is an Eddie Haskell. For every Theo, there is a Cockroach. For every Doogie Howser, there is a Vinnie. For every Zack, there is a Slater. Children who are without friends are more susceptible to gang involvement and exploitation.[35]

4. *The Crew:* Boys also benefit from a set of friends. As parents/caregivers we want to help facilitate these friendships. We want to cultivate them from within our family, neighborhood, faith sites, and community organizations. We understand the importance of peer pressure and the important role of our sons' friends. We cannot be with them all the time, but we do want to help them pick other children with goals and purpose, so their peer group will be a positive influence. The book *The Pact* illustrates how young men (in this case from the inner city), when they link together with a positive purpose and a plan, can defy the odds and avoid becoming sad statistics.[36]

5. *The Coddler:* Most boys are, sadly, taught that they cannot share their true emotions, participate in certain activities, or violate other *man rules*, which leaves many of our sons in emotional confusion and distress. The Coddler is the person who allows your son to express his true emotions without fear of being mocked and ridiculed. This is not a person that allows him to needlessly whine and not be held accountable for his actions, but provides a needed outlet for full expression of his inner emotions.

6. *The Counselor:* Just as familiarity with physical healthcare providers can help de-stigmatize this type of service, it is equally important to familiarize your son with mental healthcare professionals. A counselor can help provide a safe environment to discuss issues that may not seem outwardly pressing, but can provide the foundation for dealing with obstacles and hurdles that life may present later. Guidance counselors, social workers, and school psychologists are excellent and nonstigmatizing resources for your son.

7. *The Cube:* Today's children are more invested in "cubes" than ever before—not a Rubik's *Cube*, but rather listening to lyrics from rappers like Ice *Cube*, playing on the Game *Cube* (or other gaming system), sitting in front of the big *cube* (better known as the television), or using all the technology-based social media *cubes*. As parents/caregivers, we have to be careful about what our sons are exposed to and influenced by in this pervasive usage. Technology can certainly be a good thing, and our sons benefit from this educationally and socially; however, the dangers and risks associated with it are perhaps greater. In their book *Packaging Boyhood*, Drs. Lyn Brown, Sharon Lamb,

and Mark Tappan explain how media images are created with boys in mind as consumers, and how these images help influence their attitudes on a multitude of subjects, and most are not positive. Therefore, it is crucial that you understand what your sons are watching and listening to at home.[37] This is the friend that may not be recognized as such, but in this day and age has a tremendous amount of influence on your son.

8. *The Coolest:* This role is occupied by a big brother, godfather, cousin, uncle, or family friend. This is a person that your son believes walks on water and can help to influence him in a positive direction. This is the person who can talk to your son when no one else can. This is a person who your son calls when he knows he has messed up and needs help but is too afraid to tell you. This person may have some character flaws, but has an undeniable dedication to and affinity for your son. This is the person who can talk about issues that are uncomfortable but must be addressed. In that regard, this person is also *your* best friend.

#8 Responsibilities

Your son needs responsibilities. And this needs to be more than just keeping up with his academic studies. Boys need to learn chores, both inside the house and outside. This will foster independence and diminish gender stereotypes that keep many men so limited with respect to caregiving and homemaking. *Lack* of responsibilities in boyhood can enable a man in adulthood to think he should be taken care of by others (women), and may degrade his work ethic and motivation to go forth in his life. Here are some appropriate responsibilities for young men and boys:

- clean room
- cut the grass, shovel snow
- take out the garbage
- help out with younger siblings
- clean the bathroom
- complete homework
- launder and fold clothes
- help care for household pets
- wash the dishes.

#9 Helping Others

In the spirit of "all I really needed to know I learned in kindergarten," here is a quick list of ABC's for boys and young men to help them understand how they fit into society:

- Accept the good and the bad, the sun and the rain. Appreciate that lessons can be learned from both, like they were the same.
- Believe it is possible. Believe it can happen to you.
- Stretch your Comfort zone and know that the company you keep holds power over you.
- Disappointments come, Disappointments go, Disappointments hurt, but from Disappointments we grow.

- Enlightenment is the key to self-Efficacy. Exercise regularly.
- Never Fear a Fight. Be Flexible and Fair.
- Be Generous with your Gifts.
- Be Humble. Stay low in Humility and treat all men the same. Bring Honor to your name.
- Imagine yourself achieving your dreams. Imagine yourself dreaming a bigger dream.
- Jealousy arises in some people. Be careful who you let into your inner circle. Every America has a Benedict Arnold, every Jesus a Judas.
- Knowledge is power. Knowledge of self is invaluable.
- Listen and Learn. We have Learned the most when we Learn to Love all.
- Moderation is the key to all those who walk in the light of Magnanimity.
- Be Nice, even to those who are not nice.
- Others. Think of them more than yourself.
- There is a Purpose to your Pain. It generally comes after we have Performed Poorly. Poor Performance generally comes after we have not Properly Prepared.
- Quiet time leads to a Quiet heart. A Quiet heart helps you see clearly from the start.
- Respect. Give it and you get it back.
- Smile, but be Sincere. Learn to Slow down your world.
- Truth. Search for it. It is not hidden from you, but for you. It is the light to your journey.
- Unconquerable champion. Things may beat you and defeat you for a time, but nothing will conquer U!
- Vision. See your Victory before you even start your race.
- Wisdom is the application of knowledge.
- Xenophobia is the fear of the unknown. This fear does not allow us to solve for "X" and keeps us trapped in a small comfort zone.
- Always love You. Yield not to those same temptations.
- Never lose your Zeal for life.

#10 Continue to Grow

This last idea puts the responsibility on you to create a personalized list of what your son needs. As noted above for adults, a general list is helpful, but no one will understand your son like you. Continue to find ways that address your son's unique needs as he grows into manhood. No book or person can give you all the answers, but these resources can help you customize a plan with goals that fit for your son now and in the future.

NOTES

1. Covey, S. (1989). *The 7 habits of highly effective people*. New York: Free Press.
2. Jackson, George (Producer) & McHenry, Doug (Director) (1994). *Jason's Lyric* [motion picture]. United States: Metro Goldwyn Mayer.
3. Dyer, W. (2005). *The power of intention: Learn to co-create your world your way*. Carlsbad, CA: HayHouse.

4. Johnson, Spencer (1998). *Who moved my cheese?* New York: Penguin Putnam, Inc.
5. Phillips, B. & D'Orso, M. (1999). *Body for life.* New York: HarperCollins.
6. Schwartz, J. & Thomas, K. (2013, December 6). Health care law providing relief and frustration. *New York Times.* Retrieved from: http://www.nytimes.com/2013/12/07/us/politics/health-law-eases-some-worries-but-creates-others-in-north-carolina.html.
7. Olson, S. (2013, July 18). CDC says US life expectancy is up, which state, gender, and race living the longest? *Medical Daily.* Retrieved from: http://www.medicaldaily.com/cdc-says-us-life-expectancy-which-state-gender-and-race are-living-longest-247806.
8. Max, D.T. (2010, May). The secrets of sleep. *National Geographic.* Retrieved from: http://ngm.nationalgeographic.com/2010/05/sleep/max-text.
9. Ibid.
10. Clason, G. (1926). *The richest man in Babylon.* New York: Penguin Books.
11. Kiysaki, R.T. (2000). *Rich dad, poor dad.* New York: Warner Books Ed.
12. Stanley, T.J. & Danko, W. (1996). *The millionaire next door: The surprising secrets of America's wealthy.* New York: Gallery Books.
13. Orman, S. (2000). *9 Steps to financial freedom: Practical and spiritual steps so you can stop worrying.* New York: Three Rivers Press.
14. Hill, N. (1937). *Think and grow rich.* New York: Falls River Press.
15. Harper, H. (2008). *The wealth cure: Putting money in its place.* New York: Penguin Group.
16. Veblen, T. (1899). *The theory of the leisure class.* New York: Macmillan.
17. Pullen, R.L. (2009). *Colonoscopy.* Retrieved from: http://www.nursingcenter.com/lnc/journalarticle?Article_ID=934749.
18. Muhammad, E. (1967). *How to eat to live.* Phoenix, AZ: Secretarius MEMPS.
19. Pratt, S.G. & Matthews, K. (2004). *Super foods: Fourteen foods that will change your life.* New York: HarperCollins.
20. Smith, I. (2008). *The 4 day diet.* New York: St. Martin's Press.
21. Marx, F. (Director) (2011). *Boys to men* [documentary film]. United States: Warrior Films.
22. Perry, B. (2005). Applying principles of neurodevelopment to clinical work with maltreated and traumatized children: The nonsequential model of therapeutics. In N.B. Webb (Ed.), *Working with traumatized youth in child welfare* (pp. 27–52). New York: Guilford Press.
23. Chapman, G. (1992). *The five love languages: How to express heartfelt commitment to your mate.* Chicago, IL: Northfield Pressing.
24. Roach, T. (1995). *God's love bank.* Abilene, TX: Love Bank Enterprises Publishers.
25. Kozol, J. (1991). *Savage inequalities: Children in American schools.* New York: Crown.
26. Obiakor, F.E., Harris-Obiakor, P., & Smith, R.L. (2002). The comprehensive support model for all learners: Conceptualizations and meaning. In F.E. Obiakor, P.A. Grant, & E.A. Dooley (Eds.), *Educating all learners: Refocusing the comprehensive support model* (pp. 3–17). Springfield, IL: Thomas.
27. Mayo Clinic. *Concussions.* Retrieved from: http://www.mayoclinic.com/health/concussion/DS00320/TAB=indepth.
28. Chua, A. (2011). *Battle hymn of the tiger mom.* New York: Penguin Books.
29. Mercola, J. (2010, March 16). MSG: Is this silent killer lurking in your kitchen cabinets? Retrieved from: http://www.huffingtonpost.com/dr-mercola/msg-is-this-silent-killer_b_491502.html.
30. The Food Journal (2013, April 29). *The broad use of pesticides to produce more food.* Retrieved from: http://www.thefoodjournal.com/articles/the-broad-use-of-pesticides-to-produce-more-food.hmtl.

31. Lewis, L.B., Galloway-Gilliam, L., Flynn, G., Nomachi, J., Keener, L.C., & Sloane, D.C. (2011). Transforming the urban food desert from the grassroots up: A model for community change. *Family Community Health, 34(1S)*, S92–S101.

32. Wolfe, D. (2009). *Superfoods: The food and medicine of the future.* Berkeley, CA: North Atlantic Books.
    Family Education. *Michelle Obama tackles a national crisis—Childhood obesity.* Retrieved from: http://life.familyeducation.com/obesity/physical-education/65207.html.

34. Hitti, M. (2007, June 10). Men say they are fine and only go to the doctor when they are extremely sick. Retrieved from: http://men.webmd.com/news/20070620/why-men-skip-doctor-visits.

35. Davis, S., Jenkins, G., & Hunt R. (2002). *The pact: Three young men make a promise and fulfill a dream.* Upper Saddle River, NJ: Prentice Hall.

36. Ibid.

37. Brown, L.M., Lamb, S., & Tappan, M. (2009). *Packaging boyhood: Saving our sons from superheroes, slackers, and other media stereotypes.* New York: St. Martin's Press.

EPILOGUE

A world without violence. Would that ever happen? The future is uncertain in this regard because even though violence has waxed and waned over the course of human history, it has been a persistent part of it nevertheless. We frankly don't believe that humanity will ever rid itself of this plague. However, we do hope for a world in which the use of aggression and violence is more limited and contained. Where violence is not used—intentionally or unintentionally—to hurt others. Where males have multiple other ways to solve problems, and violence is a last resort. At this juncture in history, it seems that things are actually the opposite. Men are quite willing to impose their will on others based on an "us versus them" analysis and a perceived mandate to seek retribution, often in the defense of a narrowly defined version of masculinity.

We also believe that much of the existing violence in our world is an outcome of larger scale systemic issues. As long as there is an imbalance of power and privilege, oppressors and oppressed individuals, and unfairness, societies will continue to endure unwanted outcomes, including violence. This holds true at the nation-state level as well, where perceived threats to national security are always on the horizon and warfare is viewed as a legitimate means by which to become more secure. Therefore, the problem is much greater than the violent individual.

However, as individuals who are concerned about this problem, we must simply try to think globally while we act locally. As stated earlier in our book, the ultimate goal of an upstream or ecological approach to protecting, educating, and connecting boys and young men is to foster *sustained* violence reduction, while still honoring the positive aspects of male socialization (e.g., the provider/protector role, paternal responsibility). This could pay dividends not only on an individual level but, over time, also on a societal one in which there is less perceived need to categorize other groups of men as a dichotomous "friend or foe." Whether this shift will ultimately result in less institutional or even international unfairness and violence remains to be seen, but it seems certainly worth the effort when we consider the widening gap between rich and poor, and the relative ease by which groups or nations currently go to war—this in an era where weapons of mass destruction are more and more prevalent. The old adage applies here: "If you want peace, fight for justice."

The same way that "it takes a village to raise a child," it also takes multiple villages and multiple voices (that will not always be in agreement) to act against systemic forces that continue to discriminate against some, benefit others, and as a byproduct continue to foster violence. We (men) need to learn to listen to those who think, look, believe, and act differently than we do. We need to learn ways to achieve common goals, regardless of disagreement along the way.

It wasn't until the three of us first sat down to write a book with one voice that we realized the great challenge was to *agree* on one voice. In the end, we didn't really achieve that, but we do believe we reached a consensus about the need to decrease violence in our society, that social justice is a necessity, and that at the core men need to change the way they currently define themselves. We know there is not one way to do this, but multiple avenues and multiple voices. The Building a Better Man Project is just one of many viable options in this regard. It is incumbent on all of us in the field to work together, to recognize that our differences *are* our strength and that there is actually more that unites us than divides us. We the authors are still learning how to accept each other's truths and differences as men with very diverse backgrounds, and in the process we continue to learn how to listen and how to work together. In some small way, we hope that our own collaboration will encourage others to believe that the less violent world we all envision may actually be possible.

INDEX

Made in the USA
Lexington, KY
14 April 2018